ISIS: DEFINING THE ENEMY

HEARING

BEFORE THE

SUBCOMMITTEE ON TERRORISM, NONPROLIFERATION, AND TRADE

OF THE

COMMITTEE ON FOREIGN AFFAIRS
HOUSE OF REPRESENTATIVES

ONE HUNDRED FOURTEENTH CONGRESS

FIRST SESSION

APRIL 29, 2015

Serial No. 114–31

Printed for the use of the Committee on Foreign Affairs

Available via the World Wide Web: http://www.foreignaffairs.house.gov/ or http://www.gpo.gov/fdsys/

U.S. GOVERNMENT PUBLISHING OFFICE

94–386PDF   WASHINGTON : 2015

For sale by the Superintendent of Documents, U.S. Government Publishing Office
Internet: bookstore.gpo.gov   Phone: toll free (866) 512–1800; DC area (202) 512–1800
Fax: (202) 512–2104   Mail: Stop IDCC, Washington, DC 20402–0001

COMMITTEE ON FOREIGN AFFAIRS

EDWARD R. ROYCE, California, *Chairman*

CHRISTOPHER H. SMITH, New Jersey
ILEANA ROS-LEHTINEN, Florida
DANA ROHRABACHER, California
STEVE CHABOT, Ohio
JOE WILSON, South Carolina
MICHAEL T. McCAUL, Texas
TED POE, Texas
MATT SALMON, Arizona
DARRELL E. ISSA, California
TOM MARINO, Pennsylvania
JEFF DUNCAN, South Carolina
MO BROOKS, Alabama
PAUL COOK, California
RANDY K. WEBER SR., Texas
SCOTT PERRY, Pennsylvania
RON DeSANTIS, Florida
MARK MEADOWS, North Carolina
TED S. YOHO, Florida
CURT CLAWSON, Florida
SCOTT DesJARLAIS, Tennessee
REID J. RIBBLE, Wisconsin
DAVID A. TROTT, Michigan
LEE M. ZELDIN, New York
TOM EMMER, Minnesota

ELIOT L. ENGEL, New York
BRAD SHERMAN, California
GREGORY W. MEEKS, New York
ALBIO SIRES, New Jersey
GERALD E. CONNOLLY, Virginia
THEODORE E. DEUTCH, Florida
BRIAN HIGGINS, New York
KAREN BASS, California
WILLIAM KEATING, Massachusetts
DAVID CICILLINE, Rhode Island
ALAN GRAYSON, Florida
AMI BERA, California
ALAN S. LOWENTHAL, California
GRACE MENG, New York
LOIS FRANKEL, Florida
TULSI GABBARD, Hawaii
JOAQUIN CASTRO, Texas
ROBIN L. KELLY, Illinois
BRENDAN F. BOYLE, Pennsylvania

AMY PORTER, *Chief of Staff* THOMAS SHEEHY, *Staff Director*
JASON STEINBAUM, *Democratic Staff Director*

––––––––

SUBCOMMITTEE ON TERRORISM, NONPROLIFERATION, AND TRADE

TED POE, Texas, *Chairman*

JOE WILSON, South Carolina
DARRELL E. ISSA, California
PAUL COOK, California
SCOTT PERRY, Pennsylvania
REID J. RIBBLE, Wisconsin
LEE M. ZELDIN, New York

WILLIAM KEATING, Massachusetts
BRAD SHERMAN, California
BRIAN HIGGINS, New York
JOAQUIN CASTRO, Texas
ROBIN L. KELLY, Illinois

CONTENTS

ISIS: DEFINING THE ENEMY

WEDNESDAY, APRIL 29, 2015

House of Representatives,
Subcommittee on Terrorism, Nonproliferation, and Trade,
Committee on Foreign Affairs,
Washington, DC.

The subcommittee met, pursuant to notice, at 2 o'clock p.m., in room 2172 Rayburn House Office Building, Hon. Ted Poe (chairman of the subcommittee) presiding.

Mr. POE. The subcommittee will come to order.

Without objection, all members may have 5 days to submit statements, questions, extraneous materials for the record subject to the length and limitation in the rules.

The Middle East is a complex place. Major players weave an intricate web of support and opposition. As you can see on the screen that is on each end of the committee room—and Ambassador, I think there may be a chart that you have been furnished as well—it is hard to keep track of who supports what groups. But one thing is clear. Nobody seems to like ISIS.

Yet, despite everyone being against ISIS, we are not winning the battle against the war on ISIS. One of the reasons, I believe, is because it is not clear we understand the group very well.

It is time we called it like it is. ISIS is a radical Islamic terrorist group. The White House doesn't really like to talk about this but we cannot defeat ISIS if we do not understand who they are.

It is critical that we know what its goals are, how it seeks to achieve those goals. Even if the White House doesn't think ISIS is Islamic, ISIS does.

ISIS explains its actions and justifies them through its interpretation of the Islamic law and Islamic writings. This philosophy is reflected in its daily actions and its deadly actions.

ISIS beliefs state that Christians either must renounce their faith or embrace Islam or die. It is no coincidence then that we have seen ISIS specifically target Christians not because Christians are stealing their jobs or fighting against ISIS but merely because they are Christians.

ISIS attempts to rid Iraq of Christians that have been in Iraq since the earliest times of Christianity. The 21 Egyptians beheaded by ISIS in Libya were killed because they were Christians.

Christian towns across Syria have been destroyed by ISIS. Last Sunday, ISIS released a new video of them killing Christians, this time Christians in Ethiopia.

ISIS persecution of Christians is not letting up because its beliefs have not changed. This evil belief is what attracts many to join ISIS. Two days ago, six men from Minnesota were arrested for being recruited to the ISIS cause.

Reports indicate that there is no recruiting mastermind behind their conversation, just the belief of sharing illicit beliefs. There are a dozen more examples. Teenagers, women and fighting-age males all are heeding the call from ISIS.

The main way these recruits hear the call from ISIS is through social media. I have been raising the issue of terrorists' use of social media since 2010 when I sent a letter to YouTube asking them to change the reporting function for terrorist content.

More recently, the subcommittee held a hearing that highlighted how Twitter has exploded with ISIS propaganda and recruitment efforts. ISIS uses Twitter to broadcast its acts to the world. Twitter can do a better job policing its platform to stop terrorists from using it.

But I was happy to see that after our hearing Twitter took down 12,000 ISIS accounts and updated its rules so that even promoting terrorism is a violation. Time will tell if these new rules are enforced.

We cannot shut down ISIS' messaging. We must also counter it. To recognize that ISIS justifies its actions with Islamic verses does not mean we are at war with Islam. That is too simplistic and not realistic.

According to ISIS ideals, it also thinks the roughly 200 million Shi'a around the world should also die. Same with the heads of state of every Muslim country that has elevated man-made law above Sharia law.

What we need is a deeper understanding of what ISIS believes and to use this understanding to defeat ISIS and its philosophy.

For example, if we had a better idea of ISIS philosophy then we would better understand why people join this group. This will, in turn, give us ways to stem the flow of foreign fighters going to this terrorist group.

Another example—if we know ISIS' legitimacy is based upon establishing a caliphate that must control territory, then perhaps seizing territory from ISIS becomes a higher priority by fighting them.

There are many other possible benefits of having a better understanding of ISIS philosophy.

Finally, we need the voices of Islam who disagree with ISIS' interpretation of Islam to come and speak out against ISIS.

We need to find new ways to work with local imams, prominent well-respected Islamic scholars and like-minded NGOs here at home and abroad to get their voices heard in the Muslim world.

I think we should work with our allies to expose ISIS' half truths and show it for the charlatan that it is. ISIS has used its ideals to recruit and kill. It is time we now use and find out what that ideology is and use it against them.

I now yield to the ranking member, the gentleman from Massachusetts, for his opening statement.

Mr. KEATING. Thank you, Chairman Poe, for conducting today's hearing.

Understanding ISIS, ISIL, Daesh's ideology, how this ideology informs ISIL's goal and actions and what are the implications for the United States and its allies in countering ISIL are issues that merit serious discussion.

As the ranking member on this subcommittee and a member of the Homeland Security Subcommittee on Counterterrorism and Intelligence, I have engaged on ISIL from two perspectives—on one hand, from our efforts to counter ISIL abroad in the Middle East and on the other hand from our work to prevent terrorist acts and the flow of freedom fighters here at home.

ISIL is a unique threat, and although it rose out of the group commonly known as al-Qaeda in Iraq, its objectives and tactics differ significantly from those of al-Qaeda.

Even compared to other terrorist organizations, ISIL's tactics are especially and deliberately savage. ISIL's atrocities against its captives and religious minorities living in the territory controlled by ISIS is horrific.

Even compared to other terrorist organizations, ISIL's tactics are especially of concern to us. It is brutal, intolerant toward other faiths, and invokes its ideology to justify practices including murder, slavery and the destruction of ancient artifacts in Iraq and Syria.

But ISIL's actions are also hypocritical, for while it destroys certain pre-Islamic statues and cultural objects in the name of its ideology, it is also known to traffic in these sorts of antiquities to finance its terrorist operations.

Indeed, ISIL's members are not exclusively ideologues. Instead, I see ISIL as being made up at least loosely as three loose factions—true ideologues with an apocalyptic version of Islam, old pro-Saddam military and intelligence officers and foreign fighters from around the world.

Some of these foreign fighters are hardened fighters but many are just what the uncle of Tamerlin Tsarnaev called his nephew, one of the Boston Marathon bombers—a loser, misguided adventure seekers and young men and women who joined ISIL for some sense of power and purpose they otherwise lack.

To degrade and ultimately defeat ISIL we will have to cut off its supply of money and manpower. Specifically, we need to work with our allies to improve our efforts to prevent the flow of foreign fighters to Iraq and Syria.

We also need to do a better job of countering ISIL's messaging to potential recruits and responding to ISIL's savvy using social media.

We need to counter their communications smartly and not in a heavy-handed way that would give them legitimacy that they, frankly, do not deserve.

Further, we need to assist our allies in the region, particularly Jordan and Iraq, in containing and rolling back the territorial gains made by ISIL, for unlike al-Qaeda, ISIL still needs to control territory in order to survive.

It is my hope that today's hearing will provide some insights and constructive proposals on how the United States and its allies can enhance their efforts to counter ISIL.

Thank you, Mr. Chairman, and I yield back.

Mr. POE. The Chair will now recognize members who wish to give an opening statement for 1 minute. I would ask members to keep their statements to 1 minute.

The Chair recognizes the gentleman from California, Mr. Issa.

Mr. ISSA. Thank you, Mr. Chairman.

It is good to see you again, Ambassador. Seems like the only time we meet in safe ground is here. Otherwise, your career has been in all the places that are at the center of this discussion today and I appreciate your being here, certainly, as someone who understands the issues and the people with a level of detail that is not—even in the Near East—is not always understood.

And, Mr. Chairman, I want to thank you for holding this hearing. I certainly think understanding where we must learn not to tolerate the intolerance that leads to ISIS or for that matter the intolerance that has led to other terrorist organizations, which I think you have done a wonderful job of showing most of them on your diagram that is before us.

So, again, Ambassador, I look forward to a lively debate on all the steps that could be taken, most of which if they had been taken have failed and if they haven't been taken the question today will be why not.

I thank you and yield back.

Mr. POE. I thank the gentlemen.

The Chair recognizes the other gentleman from California, Mr. Sherman, for his opening statement.

Mr. SHERMAN. I want to commend the chair and the ranking member for their excellent selection of witnesses. One witness is particularly controversial and that is because that witness represents an organization that was formerly on the foreign terrorist organization list. Formerly.

The Japanese Government in times past carried out horrific actions, particularly against American POWs. That was then. Today, we honored the prime minister of Japan.

The prime minister was here today to promote a trade agreement that includes Vietnam, formerly an enemy of the United States. The executive branch has treated as terrorists the IRA, Sinn Fein, the African National Congress at various times. Formerly is formerly.

Second, the MEK, unlike the vast majority of witnesses, present company excepted, has actually provided Congress with startlingly interesting and useful information such as the existence of the Natanz nuclear facility.

Third, we are told that Ms. Rajavi has greater expertise on Iran than on ISIS. If we allow—if we had one witness pull out every time that witness thought that the core expertise of a fellow witness was in an area on a related issue and not the explicit subject of the hearing, we would have an awful lot of empty chairs.

And finally, the press has attacked the inclusion of the MEK in this hearing because, although the MEK has provided incredibly useful information, they tend to provide information that furthers their public policy interest.

I've been here almost 20 years. I've heard about 16,000 witnesses. I have never heard a witness that wasn't providing information to further their public policy interest.

So I look forward to hearing the witnesses here and commend you on your selection. I yield back.

Mr. POE. I thank the gentleman.

The Chair recognizes the gentleman from Pennsylvania, Mr. Perry.

Mr. PERRY. Thank you, Mr. Chairman.

President Obama declared his intention to defeat ISIS and developed a plan he believes can achieve his aims. However, I have serious concerns with the strategy, and I use the term loosely, especially because the President doesn't seem to have a clear understanding of our enemy.

In the past year, President Obama has referred to ISIS as not Islamic and as al-Qaeda's JV team—statements that caused confusion about the group and may have contributed to significant strategic errors.

Denying that the U.S. is at war with radical Islam makes it difficult to engage in a factual honest ideological debate exposing ISIS' false narrative and to empower moderate Muslim voices.

Misperceptions and the lack of understanding about ISIS have consistently led to underestimating this rapidly expanding terror group.

The reality is that ISIS is very Islamic, even if its interpretation of Islam differs from the majority of Muslims around the world, which is exactly why we should identify the enemy as what it is.

Thank you, Mr. Chairman. I yield back.

Mr. POE. The Chair now recognizes the gentleman from New York, Mr. Higgins.

Mr. HIGGINS. Thank you, Mr. Chairman, for holding this important hearing.

The understanding of ISIS' origins, motivations and ideology are of critical importance in our bid to defeat this brutal terrorist group.

ISIS' Salafi jihadist ideology is not unique among terrorist organizations. However, its brutal exploits, proficient use of social media, expansive territorial control and commitment to a pre-modern form of governance constitute a dangerous evolution that set it apart from its predecessors.

While ISIS' reliance on territorial control and governance makes it a uniquely serious threat for the United States and our partners, these attributes also represent serious vulnerability.

ISIS forces can be targeted more easily and if it continues to lose territory or its ability to govern it will have lost much of its legitimacy.

I look forward to the discussion of today's witnesses, and with that I yield back.

Mr. POE. The Chair recognizes the other gentleman from New York, Mr. Zeldin, for his opening statement.

Mr. ZELDIN. Thank you, Mr. Chairman, for holding this important hearing.

You can't defeat an enemy that you are not willing to define accurately. The President, in September 2014, outlined a strategy to defeat ISIS. That strategy needs to evolve.

In that strategy—that speech he said that he was not going to have any boots on the ground. It was going to be a different strategy than past wars in Iraq and Afghanistan. In the same exact speech he announced that he was sending 495 additional troops to Iraq.

Here, when Secretary Kerry was before the Foreign Affairs Committee recently, he said there would be no offensive action, even though right now we are engaged in kinetic air strikes.

He later clarified we still have unanswered questions as far as what kind of flexibility and resources are going to be given to that commander on the ground to actually accomplish the mission.

We are relying on Iraqi military and law enforcement to finish the job in destroying ISIS. Many of them don't even show up to work. Many of the Syrian rebels that we are relying on on Syria aren't fighting ISIS. They are going after Assad, which it wouldn't be such a bad thing if they took him out.

The strategy needs to evolve. I look forward to this hearing today to bring some more accountability not only to defining the enemy but destroying them.

Mr. POE. Without objection, all witnesses' prepared statements will be made part of the record. I ask that the witnesses keep their presentation to approximately 5 minutes.

I will introduce the first panel. Ambassador Robert Ford finished his 30-year career with the Peace Corps in the U.S. Department of State in April 2014 and now is a senior fellow at the Middle East Institute. Ambassador Ford has served the United States nobly in a lot of places that have conflict such as Algeria, Syria and Iraq.

Dr. Walid Phares, who is scheduled to testify here on the panel, is still on a plane from New York to here. So when he gets to Dulles we will be notified. But we will proceed with Ambassador Ford and your testimony at this time.

Thank you, Ambassador. Your statement will be made part of the record.

STATEMENT OF THE HONORABLE ROBERT FORD, SENIOR FELLOW, THE MIDDLE EAST INSTITUTE (FORMER U.S. AMBASSADOR TO SYRIA)

Mr. FORD. Thank you, Mr. Chairman, members of the committee. Thank you for your invitation today. It is an honor to be here to talk about the Islamic State, which is one of the biggest foreign challenges that our country and our military confronts today.

I have laid out in my written testimony some more detailed thoughts about the ideology of the Islamic State and what an understanding of that ideology would suggest in terms of our own strategies.

So in my oral testimony let me just highlight a few key points. Number one, the Islamic State's ideology comes out of a Salafi jihadi school, as Congressmen Higgins just noted.

It allows for no compromise on key elements of doctrine and practice. Let me underline that. It allows for no compromise on key elements of doctrine and practice.

According to its ideology, compromise in applying divine instruction is sin and an adherent would not want to die with that sin weighing against him.

Number two—because ultimately the Islamic State rejects compromise, it also rejects pluralism and it even rejects things like borders between states and foreign governments.

Three—in policy terms, this means that the Islamic State itself thinks that it must fight communities who reject its rule. It cannot compromise with communities that reject its rule.

It would be a sin for its leaders and its adherents to make such a compromise. So what that means is that Iran and the Shi'a may be the Islamic State's greatest immediate enemy. But we need to understand that the Islamic State also sees us as an eventual if not an immediate enemy.

It views us as an enemy to the application of its literalist interpretation of divine law across the planet. The Islamic State's ideology also creates some weaknesses that we should seek to exploit.

First, its severe literalist interpretation of governance and justice alienates a great many inhabitants of territories it controls. We have seen this, for example, in Syria and Iraq.

There will be local populations in these countries with whom we can make common cause against the Islamic State.

Secondly, this is especially true with other armed opposition groups in Syria. Those opposition groups have fought the Islamic State on the ground. I want to repeat that.

Those opposition groups have fought the Islamic State on the ground for the past 16 months. Some of them are also Salafis. The Islamic State has killed scores of Salafi fighters from other groups because those other groups refused to acknowledge the Islamic State's authority.

Remember what I said. It accepts no compromise. What that also means in practical terms is that if the Assad regime in Syria were to fall, which is an event that I judge highly unlikely anytime soon, the Islamic State would not—let me repeat, the Islamic State would not take control in Damascus.

Rather, other Syrian opposition groups, like antibodies, would rush to fight against it even harder. We should be helping anti-extremist Syrian fighters the same way we are helping the Iraqi army.

Three—we should not fall into the trap, and I have seen this discussed in some policy circles here in Washington. We should not fall into the trap of thinking that working with Iran will help fix our Islamic State problem.

The Islamic State arose in part—not entirely, but in part from longstanding grievances and fears within Sunni communities in the Levant and Iraq about growing Persian and Shi'a influence.

Working with Iran, even indirectly, will feed the Islamic State narrative and will immediately help its recruiting.

Lastly, the Islamic State's declaration of a caliphate was quite controversial within Salafi jihadi circles. Its claim to legitimacy and allegiance depends on its control of land and its ability to apply its interpretation of Sharia, of Islamic law.

Were it not to control land, were it not to be able to govern, its claim to legitimacy within those Salafi jihadi circles would be undermined, and therefore seizing ground—not just air strikes but seizing ground—needs to be an important part of our strategy.

Mr. Chairman, let me conclude there and I look forward to a good discussion.

[The prepared statement of Mr. Ford follows:]

Testimony for the Record

By Robert S. Ford

Senior Fellow at Middle East Institute and U.S. Ambassador (retired)

House Foreign Affairs Committee, Terrorism, Non-Proliferation and Trade Subcommittee

Hearing on the afternoon of April 29, 2015

Mr. Chairman, distinguished members of the Committee,

It is an honor to appear before you today to discuss the ideology of the Islamic State and how our understanding of that ideology should affect our strategy against this brutal organization.

I spent five years in Iraq, mostly at the U.S. Embassy in Baghdad, and the American effort against the Islamic State's predecessor organizations, al-Qaida in Iraq and later the Islamic State in Iraq, was a major issue for me and my colleagues. Later I served at the U.S. Embassy in Damascus when we saw the Islamic State in Iraq dispatch its elements into Syria as the unrest there became violent in the second half of 2011.

Without going now into all of the details of the Islamic State's ideology, I would like to highlight several key points:

1. The organization's establishment back in Iraq started as part of the Iraqi Sunni Arab grievances against the Iraqi Shia, and to a somewhat smaller extent the Americans, and that aggrieved Iraqi Sunni Arab community now extends to include Sunni Arab communities in Syria and Lebanon, with many sympathizers in North Africa, the Gulf and other Sunni Muslim communities.

2. The Islamic State's ideology falls within a broader category of conservative Sunni Muslim belief called "Salifi-jihadism" but it is the most extreme, and it regularly labels as heretical even Sunni Muslims who do not accept its interpretations.

In short, in its interpretations, if it makes compromises or tolerates different points of view, it is not defending God's word and hence its followers are themselves guilty of sin.

3. This inability to accept pluralism or tolerate other points of view also means, for example, that it will not accept other political institutions or borders. Its ideology

requires that the Islamic State fight enemies on all sides and prevail; long-term of acceptance of borders, for example, would be a sin in its followers' eyes.

4. The Islamic State's interpretation of Quranic text and prophetic sayings leads it to look forward to a final clash with the Western world, but the declaration made when it declared the Caliphate in 2014 highlights more the need to fight Shia whom it views as apostates.

5. The declaration by the Islamic State's leadership of a caliphate caused huge discussion and uproar among the Salafi-jihadi community, and there were many questions about whether the Islamic State -- the Caliphate -- is a legitimate effort. Criteria include whether or not the caliphate has any political capabilities to govern, whether the caliphate accentuates divisions among those fighting against the Shia and the Americans and whether the timing was proper.

6. Finally, the Islamic State's ideology demands establishment of a political entity that governs, and administers justice very much along the lines of the Muslim community immediately after the Prophet Mohammed's death. It applies very literalist interpretations and these often harken back to pre-modern forms of governance, punishment and treatment of subjugated populations.

Because the Islamic State accepts no state borders, and it believes its precepts apply universally to all people on the planet, it expects to fight us sooner or later. Right now its biggest target is the Iraqi government since that is led by Shia whom it considers apostates. And on its western front its biggest enemies are the other Syrian armed opposition groups whom it judges are apostates as well as competitors, and the Assad regime whom it perceives is just another Shia-linked apostate regime.

The administration is right to understand that we have to confront the Islamic State, and this is an organization wholly different from al-Qaida. However, if we properly understand the ideology that drives the Islamic State, we would understand that

1. It will never stop fighting in Syria and Iraq, or in other countries where it has a foothold; it might eventually seek temporary truces, but its absolutist interpretations means that eventually the Islamic State will choose to fight all other communities that do not recognize its authority.

2. Its severe, literalist interpretations of governance and justice alienate a great many of the inhabitants of territories it controls since many of those inhabitants enjoy aspects of 20th and 21st century living. We have seen this in places like Raqqa and Deir Zour in

Syria and in Mosul in Iraq (we also saw with Iraqi Anbar during the time of the Islamic State's predecessor organizations).

3. Likewise, it won't work well with other opposition groups in Iraq and Syria. It has killed Salafi fighters by the scores in Syria, including even fighters from al-Qaida. Were the Assad regime to fall -- something that is highly unlikely at present -- it is also extremely unlikely that other Syrian opposition groups would accept domination or rule by the Islamic State, and they have and have used arms to fight the Islamic State.

We therefore have an opening to find indigenuous fighters who will combat the Islamic State, although nearly all Syrians opposition figures think Assad is the number one enemy.

4. Among jurisprudents in Salafi circles, the Islamic State has vulnerability about its declaration of its being a caliphate and the long-hoped for new caliphate. If it loses territory so that it cannot govern, and its judges cannot administer its brand of justice, it loses some of the legitimacy of its claim to loyalty and allegiance.

The ground gains in Iraq are important, therefore. Air strikes, however, will not wrest control of territory - physical space - back from the Islamic State in Syria. There has to be a ground force - and I would argue strongly that it should be an indigenuous ground force.

5. Perhaps oddly, the Islamic State has attracted many younger ideologues within the Salifi-jihad sphere. We shouldn't place huge hopes on establishment Muslim establishments like Egypt's Azhar as being influential with these younger writers and thinkers. Rather, younger thinkers and imams who have both scholarly credentials and street credibility will best be able to undermine Islamic State standing among some of its followers.

6. Finally, as we and friends fight against the Islamic State, it is extremely important to remember the original context - aggrieved Sunni Muslim communities in places like Lebanon, Syria and Iraq who are angry at and afraid of Iran and the Arab Shia. If we ally with Iran against the Islamic State, directly or indirectly, we play into the Islamic State's narrative and will help its recruitment.

Thank you again for your invitation to testify before the subcommittee and I look forward to any further comments or questions you might have.

Mr. POE. Thank you, Ambassador, for succinctly outlining the issue before us.

What is the doctrine of ISIS? You mentioned that there were two issues. They won't compromise. Compromise is sin. What is the doctrine?

Mr. FORD. The Islamic State's leadership and its adherents, the ones that are ideologically driven—and I rush to add here, Mr. Chairman, that not everyone that fights under the banner of the Islamic State is probably ideologically driven—I think a great many, especially in Syria, are driven by more mundane things like salaries and access to food and war supplies.

But for the ideologically driven among them, their goal is to apply their interpretation—emphasize that, their interpretation—of divine law, Sharia, on the planet.

And they—because they do not accept borders, any borders, they believe that it is to be applied universally to all mankind and those who resist must, in the end, submit and—either submit or be killed.

Mr. POE. Submit or die?

Mr. FORD. Right. Now, can I add one thing on this? I have seen a great deal of discussion about the Islamic State and Christians.

The doctrine—the doctrine is that Christians must either convert or submit, and submit in this case means pay taxes, which in Islamic law is called jizya, or they face death, too. So it is convert, pay the tax or they can leave—they can go somewhere else—or they will be killed.

Mr. POE. Convert, pay your taxes or die?

Mr. FORD. Or leave, yes.

Mr. POE. Or leave.

Mr. FORD. So what I saw, for example, people who claimed to be from the Islamic State in Libya, where they murdered the Egyptian Coptic Christians and then the Ethiopian Christians, I think that falls well outside even the Islamic State's interpretation.

For example, in Syria they allowed Christians to stay but they insisted that they pay that tax—the jizya.

Mr. POE. Let me move on to some other comments that you made. Their leadership—let us use them. And I understand people are joining ISIS for different reasons. They are not all united on the reason that they are there.

But it is their interpretation of what they see as divine law that drives their process of doctrine and then drives their process of compromise or refusing to compromise.

I want to talk about the compromise part. That means compromise with anybody else—is that correct—let us say other Muslim beliefs, other Muslim philosophies about religion or the Koran.

Mr. FORD. Correct. They believe that their interpretation is the only valid one and that is why they have murdered scores and scores of even other Salafis in places like Syria.

They are by far the most extreme, which is why in a place like Syria, Mr. Chairman, you have some Salafis fighting other Salafis.

Mr. POE. A couple more questions with my time remaining. One thing that you mentioned that makes them different than all these other terrorist groups that are listed on this chart—and you need a flow chart to keep up with them—in the whole world——

Mr. FORD. That is quite a chart, Mr. Chairman.

Mr. POE. Well, you can keep it. There is no pride of authorship. They control and desire to control land. Unlike al-Qaeda and the Taliban, who hide in caves and run out and do mischief and then run back to their caves, ISIS is up front.

They want to control swathes—big areas—and get bigger to have a caliphate there in Syria, Iraq and move in different directions. Is that what makes them different than other terrorist organizations?

Mr. FORD. That is one of the most distinguishing features of the Islamic State is this drive, this insistence by the Islamic State, to actually create a governing entity and not just a terrorist entity but a real live governing organization with a bureaucracy, with a military, that collects taxes, that operates court systems openly.

That is what is different, and their declaration of that, Mr. Chairman, was quite controversial within Salafi jihadi circles.

A lot of other Salafis said it is not time. It is premature. Or they said you don't actually control the land and you won't be able to do it and so you are full of baloney. Others said your doing so will simply increase divisions among the Salafis and therefore it is unwise.

So that is a point of vulnerability—that declaration of the caliphate, this issue of controlling land—is a real vulnerability within their own school of Salafi jihad Islam.

Mr. POE. Try to get two quick questions, maybe quick answers back. How big is ISIS, number wise?

Mr. FORD. In terms of total numbers of people that live under its control, happily or unhappily, probably a couple of million.

The big cities in Iraq that are under its control are Fallujah and Mosul and probably have a population of 1.5 to 2 million. Then on the Syrian side, maybe another million.

Mr. POE. And ISIS has made it clear by their actions and their beliefs and their rhetoric that Iran is an enemy of ISIS because of their different doctrine and philosophies of the Iranian Government. And you mentioned it would be—would it be foolish for the United States to try to side with Iran trying to fight ISIS? Is that what you were saying?

Mr. FORD. Exactly. That plays into their efforts to recruit by saying there is an American-Iranian conspiracy to put down the Sunnis and we are the ones fighting it.

Mr. POE. All right. Thank you, Mr. Ambassador. I will yield to the ranking member, Mr. Massachusetts.

Mr. KEATING. I like that. Makes me sound like some kind of bodybuilder.

Mr. POE. I called you something different last week, if you remember. Go ahead.

Mr. KEATING. Thank you, Mr. Chairman. Thank you, Mr. Texas.

I just want to deal with the issue, initially, of foreign fighters and there are some written reports—I will only go that far in commenting on them—that there might be as many as 22,000 upwards in terms of foreign fighters.

They are the people they are putting on the front line, many times for suicide attacks and the most vicious attacks in that regard. So a couple of things.

Number one, Turkey has shown, some initial hesitancy at least, in working to degrade and defeat ISIL. Foreign fighters continue to pass through Turkey. What can the United States and its allies do to further engage Turkey, and what more can Turkey do to guard its borders so that it can't be used as a conduit for these foreign fighters as much as it has been?

Mr. FORD. Congressman, the Turks do have a border problem and it is causing problems for us, too. They need more manpower along that border because these are—let us be frank—they are ancient smuggling routes.

There are lots of little goat paths—there are lots of little donkey paths that have been there for centuries and they need to be shut down.

There is not a fence along the entire 500-mile Syrian-Turkish border and there is not a fence along the Iraq-Turkish border either.

So it is a question of devoting more resources. The Turks have also asked for greater cooperation in terms of sharing the names of extremists moving around. I think that will help but that is not sufficient. There is a strong need for actual control—physical control of the border.

The other thing I would just say, and I think this is really important, I was in Turkey recently at the end of January and beginning of February.

The Turks have real doubts about the utility of a policy that focuses on combatting the Islamic State without also dealing with and removing the Bashar al-Assad government, which they believe fuels the recruitment to the Islamic State.

Their argument would be something like this. You can bomb and kill 50 of them and they will recruit 45, 48 or 50 the next day because they want to fight Bashar al-Assad. So the strategy that the American administration has laid out, in the Turkish view, is inadequate.

Mr. KEATING. I see. Also, just looking at our European allies in this regard, what can they do that they are not doing now to help stem the flow of foreign fighters?

Mr. FORD. Couple of comments on that. First, I think many of our European friends are genuinely concerned about the size of the foreign fighter flow. You mentioned a 22,000 number. I have seen numbers like that.

I know, for example, that the French and the Belgians are exceptionally concerned about the numbers of their citizens that are going. And so, in a sense, you have to deal with it on two levels.

One is just a pure intelligence and security effort to block movements, whether they be out of Europe or coming back into Europe. And then the second is, they need people within the Muslim communities of those countries themselves to be explaining to potential recruits why joining the Islamic State is not only wrong morally, but will also land them in serious trouble.

Mr. KEATING. Other groups, including affiliates in Afghanistan, Algeria, Egypt, Libya as well as Boko Haram in Nigeria, have significantly pledged to ISIL as well. What are the operational and financial relationships between these organizations, and do ISIL leaders exert command and control in any way over these groups?

Mr. FORD. There have been lots of little Salafi splinter groups that have announced their allegiance to the Islamic State, although some others have pointedly declined to do so in places like Algeria.

The two big ones that have pledged allegiance are Libya and in the Sinai Peninsula. Those are the two most serious.

On the Libya side, I am not aware that there is much command and control. I rather doubt that. But there certainly has been some sharing of information in terms of how to use social media and how to do filming.

If you saw, for example, that terrible film where the Egyptian Christians were marched onto the beach and then murdered, that bore a very frightening resemblance to videos that have come out of places like Iraq and Syria, and the same in Sinai.

So there certainly are some kinds of links but I don't know if it extends to command and control. With respect to financial, Congressman, I just can't say one way or the other. I don't know.

Mr. KEATING. Well, thank you, Ambassador. I yield back.

Mr. POE. The Chair recognizes the gentleman from California, Mr. Issa.

Mr. ISSA. Thank you, Mr. Chairman.

Ambassador, bios are a wonderful thing, especially when they link us back to the early days of the Afghan initiative after 9/11. At that time, the then Bush administration was focused on Afghanistan and the Taliban-supporting al-Qaeda.

We have certainly morphed a long way during the second half of your career and my entire career in Congress together. Today, that complex chart that I will hold up one more time and say it isn't nearly complex enough for the problem——

Mr. FORD. I hope there is not a test on that chart later.

Mr. ISSA. Well, if——there are a whole bunch of lines that should go both ways for opposed, too. But before we modify that, Ambassador, we were overly simplistic in 2001 when we viewed the Middle East.

At that point you were halfway through your career. You were an expert in Near East, Middle East, and a little bit of Africa. Now, today, we are a little more aware of the complexity.

We understand the real struggles between various power groups—the former Ottoman Empire in Turkey and their not wanting to acquiesce to other powers—obviously, Persian expansion to regain their historic position, and Saudi Arabia's control of Mecca and Medina.

I am not trying to give a lecture here. I will bring this to a close. These odd alliances that often—you explained caliphates—but, of course, the idea that an Alawite minority in Syria, somewhat Shi'a in its nature, could dominate the area and in fact support both Shi'a and Sunni operations against Israel is longstanding and has been ignored.

So what I want to do in the limited time after this little diatribe of history is ask you specifically, Syria seems to be one of our most complex areas.

We know that everybody in Syria either is or could be on the wrong side because we, obviously, know that Assad is aligned with Iran. We know that many of the Sunnis are involved with ISIS and, as you said, there is a real question about what after Assad.

So let me just go through two or three quick points and you can take as much time as the chairman will give you afterwards.

The potential outcome if Assad falls is one area, because although he has shown a resilience it is not a forever situation in any of these countries.

Secondly, the effects of a no-fly zone both on the long-term strategy of, if you will, bringing peace of some sort to Syria with or without Assad leaving and its effect on refugees.

And then the last one, which is the one I alluded to in this long question—how would you suggest we find and define and be comfortable in what the administration calls the, if you will, the moderate Free Syrian Army forces?

How do you find those groups when there seem to be more people in the two other groups that we say we oppose? And thanks for taking notes on that. If there is time left, we will go to Yemen.

Mr. FORD. I think Syria is just the hardest nut. It is just the hardest nut to crack, very tough. With respect to your questions, I think it is very unlikely, as I said, that Assad's regime is going to collapse tomorrow or the next day.

It is getting weaker but I don't think it is about to collapse. But if we think—if we stretch out this—where it is going in this long horrible war of attrition, were the regime to finally be worn down what you would have is you would just have more groups fighting for control of the capital and you might end up with a situation where different opposition groups control different neighborhoods of Damascus. The Islamic State might control some but they wouldn't control it all.

Mr. ISSA. Right. And in that vein, what would be the effects on Christians, a rather large minority in the region, since Assad is effectively the protectorate of Christians?

Mr. FORD. Well, I don't—I wouldn't call Bashar al-Assad the protector of the Christians. He likes to call himself that but his forces have bombed plenty of churches, too.

Mr. ISSA. Sure.

Mr. FORD. So the effect on Christians, like the effect on all Syrians, would be really bad because the fighting would just get worse. We will have a huge surge of refugees out of Damascus so——

Mr. ISSA. Which brings us to the other two points, the no-fly zone, and where do you find moderates?

Mr. FORD. Yes. With respect to the no-fly zone, this is a tough one. Where I am on this now, Congressman, is a no-fly zone could help but not just without thought and a strategy.

The no-fly zone—we had a no-fly zone in Iraq and it lasted 12 years and it only ended when U.S. troops went into Baghdad. So I don't think we want to do another 12-year no-fly zone over Syria.

So the real question is, can you use a no-fly zone to get to the political settlement that we want? And that requires then that in return for our doing a no-fly zone, the opposition—the Syrian opposition—is going to reach out to elements that now support the Assad regime and say, hey, there is a third choice.

It doesn't have to be the Islamic State or Assad. There is a moderate third choice. Work with us on that.

I have to be honest. I don't think the Syrian opposition has done a very good job of that. And the other part of that is if we are going to do it the quid pro quo really needs to be from the Turks—you will put the resources on that border and shut it down so that we don't have Islamic State and al-Qaeda elements moving back and forth over the order to get food, to get medical care, to travel, whatever it is.

So if we are going to do a no-fly zone, Congressman, we need to leverage that to get things that we need out of the other side.

With respect to your question about how do you find moderates in the Syrian armed opposition, that is a——

Mr. POE. If you would, Ambassador, try to keep it brief.

Mr. FORD. Yes. The main thing is, Congressman, there are moderates. There always have been moderates. They need support. There is a competition for recruits between moderates and extremists. We need to empower the moderates to be able to recruit better.

Mr. ISSA. Thank you, Mr. Chairman.

Mr. POE. The Chair recognizes the gentleman from New York, Mr. Higgins.

Mr. HIGGINS. Thank you, Mr. Chairman.

Ambassador, ISIS seeks death and destruction to anyone who does not believe as they do. They have a presence in Syria. They have a presence in Iraq. They are expanding to North Africa and they appear to be on the move.

What is the historical relationship between ISIS and al-Qaeda? ISIS is an outgrowth of al-Qaeda—a radical outgrowth of al-Qaeda, I presume, but I need your clarification on that.

Mr. FORD. The Islamic State is actually the offspring of al-Qaeda and in particular the al-Qaeda in Iraq organization. But originally al-Qaeda in Iraq was not thinking about setting up a state.

Over a period of years, really, between 2006 and 2013, al-Qaeda in Iraq more and more took on the idea of creating a state, of creating a caliphate. But originally it was loyal to bin Laden and Zawahiri and the real split that now exists between the Islamic State and al-Qaeda is mainly over this issue of a state.

Mr. HIGGINS. Okay. The—in the Middle East or in the continent of Africa is there—are there instances of al-Qaeda and ISIS in open conflict?

Mr. FORD. I am not aware of al-Qaeda and Islamic State elements fighting each other in North Africa or in sub-Saharan Africa. I have not seen that. But there has certainly been evidence of that in abundance in Lebanon and in Syria.

Mr. HIGGINS. Okay. So there is, clearly, the potential for more of that open conflict between those two groups. ISIS is—wants to be ever present. ISIS wants to control territory and expand its control of that territory yet they don't appear at the moment to pose an existential threat to the United States. Al-Qaeda has been more explicit about that. Is that an accurate statement?

Mr. FORD. The Islamic State has said plenty of blood-curdling things against the United States and it has threatened the United States on any number of social media messages.

Mr. HIGGINS. Okay.

Mr. FORD. I wouldn't call it an existential threat but it is certainly a terrorist threat, absolutely, and I think we have to take them at their word, Congressman, that if they could reach out and strike us they would.

Mr. HIGGINS. Okay. Would you—would you agree that ISIS is a product of decades of failed governance in the Arab world and of the hijacking of Arab Islam—kind of a toxic mix?

Mr. FORD. Absolutely, that is part of it. For example, there was a really good article in November of last year in the New York Times about Tunisians who were going to the Islamic State-held territories in Syria.

Tunisia has a really good middle class. It has suffered but it is still a strong middle class with Mediterranean influences. And yet thousands of Tunisians have gone over to the Islamic State, and why is that?

And the main reason is there are frustrations among many young Tunisians about corruption, lack of opportunity, bad economic opportunities. And so one element of the Islamic State appeal—not the only element but one element of the appeal—is its claim to good governance.

Mr. HIGGINS. Yes. You said in your opening statement that ISIS adopts a policy through their ideology of no compromise—compromise is sin. It rejects pluralism and it has a presence in an area of the world that is highly pluralistic and it rejects borders.

How do you combat ISIS and their expansion in this part of the world?

Mr. FORD. It is really important to seize territory because it defines itself as a state with a bureaucracy and an organization. Therefore ground forces, and I would strongly argue not for American ground forces but for indigenous ground forces in Iraq and Syria, elsewhere, Lebanon. I think that is the way to combat it ultimately.

Mr. HIGGINS. Yes, but I suppose my point is this. Without compromise, there is no negotiated settlement to this thing anywhere, anytime, and therefore they have to be destroyed.

Mr. FORD. Exactly.

Mr. HIGGINS. So, you know, the strategy is then, and we discuss a lot about where these recruits are coming from. I don't think there is enough emphasis on why they are coming and I suppose it is a more complicated question with a complicated response to it. But it seems like there is one objective here, and I suppose the question becomes how best you accomplish that.

Mr. FORD. You want to strangle it on a variety of different levels, Congressman, whether that be recruitment, financing, access to the media, which ties into recruitment and financing, and control of territory.

For sure undermining its ability to recruit is extremely important which is why I talked about not playing into the Iran idea.

Mr. HIGGINS. Okay. I yield back. My time is expired.

Mr. POE. The Chair recognizes the gentlemen from Pennsylvania, Mr. Perry.

Mr. PERRY. Thank you, Mr. Chairman.

Ambassador Ford, good to see you again. The last time we spoke was regarding the red line in Syria prior to Assad crossing the red line and if you recall my questioning was what our range of options might be.

And so that kind of colors the context of my thinking regarding the administration in my opening statement, et cetera.

With that in mind, I think that you may have alluded to the fact that the administration is right to understand that we have to confront the Islamic State and that this is an organization wholly different from al-Qaeda. I think throughout the course of the discussion you have kind of buttressed that claim.

As an individual who has worked in the current administration and maybe understands better than some of us on the outside that are casual spectators and frustrated spectators, why do you think, if you would proffer an opinion, the administration, the President in particular, it doesn't seem like he understands the threat that ISIS poses or at least his actions don't reflect that. Would you comment on that?

Mr. FORD. I think the administration actually is doing not so bad on Iraq in fighting the Islamic State in Iraq. It is going to be a slow effort but ground has been taken back, and although it is not an easy battle, I think there is progress.

On the Syria side, Congressman, I think the strategy of simply trying to arm one element of Syrian fighters and sending them into the Islamic State without looking at the broader conflict in the end will not be adequate.

There is this—Congress voted for it—$500 million program to train the new Syrian force—5,000, 10,000, maybe 15,000 if they are lucky—to go in over the next couple of years and fight the Islamic State.

I personally doubt very much that that will be an effective way to do it because it won't address the recruitment problem.

Mr. PERRY. So let me clarify because maybe I wasn't clear. I am not talking about the borders of Iraq and Syria and what is occurring there so much as the ideology, as I see it, that is not only pervasive to the region but pervasive around the globe.

And when I see that we have leaders come to the White House to have a summit and a discussion of what comes out of it is some kind of view that the terror movement is not embedded in an ideology but in socio-economic disparities I wonder if I am, and the rest of the world, are completely wholly off base—or the administration is missing the mark because one of us must be.

I mean, when you think that—you know, would you say that Osama bin Laden had economic issues that drove him? I mean, he was a wealthy man, and Ayman al-Zawahiri is—I think he is an eye surgeon, right?

I mean, these are not people without means. So why would we focus on the—I understand from a recruitment standpoint it might have a component to it. But we are talking about leaving your home as a teenager to go cut people's heads off and live a life of great hardship.

Mr. FORD. I put it like this, Congressman. For every one Osama bin Laden or every one Ayman al-Zawahiri there are probably 50 young Tunisians, young Syrians, young Iraqis who are not necessarily joining because they are ideologically driven but because they are angry at the world.

They don't have economic opportunity. They have been disenfranchised. They are sick of corruption and so the Islamic State is——

Mr. PERRY. There is a lot of Americans that feel that way that have nothing to do with it but——

Mr. FORD. Well——

Mr. PERRY [continuing]. But we don't go doing things like the Islamic State does.

Mr. FORD. The good news is, Congressman, we have a much more responsive political system than most Arab countries do. So those grievances are real and they drive a lot of the very broad Islamist movement in the region including the Salafi jihadi element among them, and my experience in the administration is that they focus on that broader problem——

Mr. PERRY. But we are not—we can find jobs in this country for people.

Mr. FORD [continuing]. Which the Islamists——

Mr. PERRY. We are talking about getting jobs in those countries for people as a solution set to the spread of this scourge. It is so counterintuitive and seems, quite honestly, it seems imbecilic.

Mr. FORD. Actually, Congressman, I don't agree. I think that were socioeconomic conditions better in many Arab countries the——

Mr. PERRY. So how do you explain the foreign fighters from America going there?

Mr. FORD. The foreign fighters from America are a tiny minority.

Mr. PERRY. Regardless——

Mr. POE. Excuse me. The gentleman's time has expired.

Mr. PERRY. Thank you, Mr. Chairman.

Mr. POE. The Chair will recognize the gentleman from New York, Mr. Zeldin.

Mr. ZELDIN. Thank you, Mr. Chairman.

I guess just picking right where Mr. Perry is leaving off, Ambassador Ford, if you were sitting in the Oval Office and President Obama was asking you for advice as to how to evolve the strategy to better defeat the threat, what would you tell him?

Mr. FORD. Find indigenous groups that will take the lead in combatting the Islamic State in North Africa, in Syria, in Lebanon, in Iraq—indigenous. The American role should be supportive but they need, A, to find indigenous fighters and B, they need to address root causes. Let me give you an example.

Mr. ZELDIN. What if you can't find indigenous forces?

Mr. FORD. Well, but I think you can and I think, frankly, if you put the resources out there you can develop the moderate forces.

Can I give you an example of what I am talking about? This is a widely known story in Syria, frankly, is where the capital of the Islamic State is now in Raqqa. So there is a soccer player named Abdul Baset al-Sarout.

He is a soccer player, well known in Syria. He joined the Islamic State after he had been fighting off the outside regime for 2 years at home and saw people bombed, et cetera, starved because of the regime's brutality. He ended up joining the Islamic State.

Syrian activists I know talked to him in January—the families know each other—and said, ''Why would you join an awful organization like the Islamic State?''

What he said was, ''How dare you talk to me about human rights and democracy when you people in the West did nothing to help us when we were being bombed and ravaged by the brutal Assad regime—how dare you lecture me.''

That is what I mean, Congressman. We have to deal with the root causes of the conflict in a place like Syria or a place like Iraq.

Mr. ZELDIN. Well, you know, Ambassador, the—I don't know if we really have enough—if there is enough patience where eventually we are going to be able to turn the tide on ISIS. I think that we all need to be much more on our game and when I say ''we'' I mean, obviously, not just the United States of America.

Now, President Obama doesn't have the military experience that his two-star general on the ground has. You know, no disrespect to him. President Bush before him, President Clinton before him, you know, they don't have six, seven tours under their belt of commanding troops on the ground.

Right now, we have thousands of American service members on the ground in Iraq. We had generals before our Foreign Affairs Committee hearing last week and we were asking what kind of flexibility does that two-star have on the ground. We asked if he knows where Abu Bakr al-Baghdadi is and if he can send a Navy SEAL team to execute a well-planned mission at night under the cover of darkness to take out the leader of ISIS; or if there was great actionable intelligence where we knew where there was, you know, a boatload of computers, for example. We asked what kind of flexibility does this two-star general have, and the general's answer back to me was reading a paragraph essentially saying that the two-star general can make a recommendation.

Now, when I am at events around my district and elsewhere and I say who is in charge of the surge in Iraq at the beginning of 2007, everyone says Petraeus, Petraeus, Petraeus.

How many of you know who the two-star general is who is in charge of our forces on the ground today?

I have asked that question to Members of Congress and they don't know the answer to that, and that two-star general doesn't have the flexibility that they need to accomplish their mission to defeat the threat.

Now, everything is being micromanaged in the White House. They send an authorization for the use of military force to Congress. We are expected to sign off on it to send our service members overseas.

Right now, the 82nd Airborne Division is preparing to go to Iraq. We want to know that we are sending them off to succeed and not fail and to actually defeat the threat.

So what may be happening right now, you know, you might have examples in Iraq, for example, of where we are degrading a threat, taking out some of their command and control, and killing some of their bad guys.

We need to kill ISIS. We need to destroy them. The whole degrading thing—if we measure success whether or not we kill a few of the bad guys but meanwhile their ranks continue to grow—they become billions of dollars richer.

Meanwhile, we are negotiating a nuclear arms race—a nuclear deal with Iran—that might trigger a nuclear arms race in the Middle East.

I am concerned that this President's strategy is not evolving quick enough to actually defeat the threat and the people on the ground don't have the ability that they need to take the action that will actually take out leadership when the opportunity presents itself.

I asked that general to clarify. I was asking him a different question and, again, he was reading the same exact paragraph that all he could do was make a recommendation.

So here we are—we are facing a real threat that if we don't defeat them overseas—we will be facing them here at home. We are literally—over the course of the last few weeks we have gone after people who are now becoming self-radicalized U.S. citizens who consider themselves to be citizens of the Islamic State.

I believe that the President's strategy needs to evolve. We know what the threat is. Now we need to take it out.

I yield back the balance of my time.

Mr. POE. I thank the gentleman from New York.

I want to thank Ambassador Ford, and Dr. Phares, glad to see that your flight finally made it. We are in the middle of a vote on the House floor. It is one vote and members have left and I assume they will come back.

But we will start—we will have your testimony, Dr. Phares, and Madam Rajavi's testimony when that vote is over with.

Ambassador Ford, you do not need to stay. I don't want to hold you up. Probably that is not a good word to use. As a former judge, I shouldn't use the word hold up, and you are welcome to stay or leave, whichever you prefer.

But we will be in recess until the vote is over with—5 minutes after the vote is over—and then we will have the testimony from our other two witnesses. So the subcommittee is in recess.

[Recess.]

Mr. POE. The subcommittee will come to order.

We have two other witnesses to testify. Ms. Maryam Rajavi is the president-elect of the National Council of Resistance of Iran.

Ms. Rajavi has appeared before many national parliaments in Europe and has published a book entitled ''Women Against Islamic Fundamentalism.''

We also have Dr. Phares. Once again, thank you for getting here no matter what it took. Dr. Phares is the co-secretary general of the Transatlantic Legislative Group on Counterterrorism.

Dr. Phares is also a professor of global strategies in Washington and has been an advisor to the U.S. House of Representatives Caucus on Counterterrorism since 2007. And before our next witness testifies, I would ask that all spectators be seated in the courtroom or in—sorry, that was a slip from the old days—in the committee room—I used to be a judge—in the committee room. So spectators be seated, please, or leave the court—or leave the room. Thank you.

I think we have the electronics working, and Madam Rajavi, we welcome you to the Subcommittee on Terrorism, Nonproliferation, and Trade.

I don't know if you heard that or not but welcome to the Subcommittee on Terrorism, Nonproliferation, and Trade and the subcommittee is ready to hear your testimony.

STATEMENT OF MS. MARYAM RAJAVI, PRESIDENT-ELECT, NATIONAL COUNCIL OF RESISTANCE OF IRAN

[The following testimony was delivered via teleconference.]

Ms. RAJAVI. Mr. Chairman, ranking member, distinguished members of the committee, thank you for giving me this opportunity to talk about this issue.

Today, Islamic fundamentalism and extremism under the name of ISIS or Shi'ite paramilitary groups have turned into a global threat.

Islamic fundamentalism emerged as a threat to peace and security when Khomeini stole the leadership of a popular revolution in 1979 and established a religious dictatorship.

The Iranian regime has served as the main source of this ominous phenomenon in the region and across the world. The primary objective of Islamic fundamentalists, including ISIS, is to establish an Islamic caliphate and enforce Sharia law.

They recognize no borders. Aggressiveness and violence are two common features of Sunni and Shi'ite extremists. As such, searching for moderates among them is an illusion.

In 1993, we published a book, ''Islamic Fundamentalism: The New Global Threat,'' warning about this threat and identifying its epicenter in Tehran. We said the mullahs sought to obtain nuclear weapons, to export fundamentalism and guarantee their own existence.

Unfortunately, little if anything was done to prevent the export of fundamentalism. Experience shows that in the absence of a firm policy vis-à-vis Tehran regime, there will be destructive consequences.

Unfortunately, failure to stop the Iranian regime's post-2003 meddling in Iraq which led to occupy that country and further spreading fundamentalism.

Similarly, crimes committed by Bashar al-Assad in Syria and the massacre and exclusion of Sunnis in Iraq by Maliki coupled with Western silence empowered ISIS. I emphasize that the mullahs' regime is not part of any solution to current crisis. It is, indeed, the heart of the problem.

The people of Iran, indeed, call the mullahs' regime godfather of ISIS and other fundamentalist groups. The ultimate solution to this problem is regime change by the Iranian people and resistance.

This regime is extremely fragile. As evident during the 2009 uprising, the overwhelming majority of the Iranian people demanded regime change. The regime's show of force is hollow and a result of weak Western policy.

Owing to the pivotal role of the People's Mojahedin Organization of Iran as a democratic Muslim movement, the Iranian resistance has established itself the antithesis to Islamic fundamentalism. We believe in separation of religion and state, gender equality, respect for rights of religious and ethnic minorities, a democratic and non-nuclear Iran. The following practical steps are necessary to achieve this goal.

One, expel the Quds Force from Iraq and end the Iranian regime's influence in that country.

Two, enable full participation of Sunnis in power sharing and arm Sunni tribes to provide security for their communities.

Three, assist Syria's moderate opposition and people to end Assad's regime and establish democracy in that country. Four, recognize the Iranian people's aspirations to overthrow the mullahs and ending inaction vis-à-vis the gross human rights violations in Iran.

Five, provide protection for and uphold the rights of members of Iran's organized opposition, the PMOI, in Camp Liberty in Iraq.

Six, empower the true democratic and tolerant Islam to counter fundamentalist interpretations of this religion.

And seven, block all pathways for the mullahs' regime to acquire nuclear weapons.

But let me finish by a quote from America's first President, George Washington: ''The harder the conflict, the greater the triumph.''

Thank you very much, Mr. Chairman.

[The prepared statement of Ms. Rajavi follows:]

Text of Testimony by Mrs. Maryam Rajavi,
The President-elect of the National Council of Resistance of Iran

Submitted to:

The House Foreign Affairs Committee,
Subcommittee on Terrorism, Non-Proliferation and Trade

April 29, 2015

Mr. Chairman, Ranking Member,
Distinguished members of the Committee,

Thank you for giving me this opportunity to speak to you.

Today, Islamic fundamentalism and extremism, in the name of ISIS or Shiite paramilitary groups, have launched a vicious onslaught against territories spanning from East Asia to the southern and eastern shores of the Mediterranean, sparing neither the Americas nor Europe.

For 36 years, we have resisted a religious tyranny, driven by Islamic fundamentalism, and fought for democracy in Iran.

Before getting into the details, allow me to briefly touch upon a few points:

1. Islamic fundamentalism and extremism emerged as a threat to regional and global peace and tranquility after a religious dictatorship (based on the principle of the *velayat-e faqih*, or absolute rule of the clergy) came to power in Iran in 1979. Since then, the regime in Tehran has acted as the driving force for, and the epicenter of, this ominous phenomenon regionally and worldwide.

2. The primary objective of fundamentalism is to establish an Islamic Empire (or Caliphate) and enforce Sharia law by force. It neither recognizes any boundaries nor differentiates between Sunnis and Shiites. Aggressiveness and the penchant for violence primarily characterize Islamic fundamentalism. As such, searching for moderates among its adherents is an illusion.

3. In 1993, we published a book entitled, "Islamic Fundamentalism; the New Global Threat,"[1] warning about this menace and identifying its epicenter as Tehran. We reiterated that the clerical regime sought to acquire the nuclear bomb in order to export its reactionary ideology and to guarantee its own survival. Regrettably, this threat was not taken seriously. The experience of the past three decades shows that

---

[1] Mohammad Mohaddessin, "Islamic Fundamentalism: The New Global Threat", 1st edition, (Seven Locks Press: 1993). Available at: http://www.amazon.com/Islamic-Fundamentalism-New-Global-Threat/dp/092976532X/ref=sr_1_12?s=books&ie=UTF8&qid=1429620723&sr=1-12&keywords=islamic+fundamentalism

in the absence of a firm policy vis-à-vis the regime in Tehran, the world will face destructive consequences.

4. Unfortunately, the failure to thwart the Iranian regime's post-2003 meddling in Iraq enabled it to gradually occupy that country, propelling the unprecedented spread of extremism. Similarly, the atrocities perpetrated by (the Islamic Revolutionary Guards Corps') Quds Force in Syria and Iraq (to prop up Tehran's puppets, Bashar al-Assad and Nuri al-Maliki), and the massacre and the exclusion of Sunnis, coupled with Western silence, empowered ISIS.

5. I reiterate that the mullahs' regime is not part of any solution as we attempt to deal with Islamic fundamentalism; it is indeed the heart of the problem.

The ultimate solution to this problem is regime change by the Iranian people and Resistance. This regime is extremely fragile and vulnerable. As evident during the 2009 uprising, the overwhelming majority of the Iranian people yearn for fundamental change, i.e. ending the theocratic regime and the establishment of democracy.

The regime's show of force is hollow and a consequence of feeble Western policy. It is intended to mask the mullahs' underlying inability to meet the demands of millions of Iranians in the 21st century.

Owing to the pivotal role of the People's Mojahedin Organization of Iran (PMOI/MEK) as a democratic Muslim movement, the Iranian Resistance has established itself as the antithesis to Islamic fundamentalism.

We can and we must defeat Islamic fundamentalism, whether the Shiite or the Sunni variants of it. Forming an international coalition and taking the following practical steps are indispensable to achieve this goal:

1. Expel the Quds Force from Iraq thus ending the Iranian regime's influence in that country. Enable genuine participation of the Sunnis in power sharing and arm Sunni tribes to empower them to provide security for their communities;
2. Assist Syria's moderate opposition and people to end Assad's tyrannical rule and establish democracy in that country;
3. Recognize the Iranian people's aspirations to overthrow the mullahs' regime and end inaction vis-à-vis the flagrant abuses of human rights in Iran. Provide protection for, and uphold the rights of, the residents of Camp Liberty (members of the PMOI/MEK) in Iraq;
4. Empower the genuine, democratic, and tolerant Islam to counter fundamentalist interpretations of this religion; and
5. Block all pathways for the Iranian regime to acquire nuclear weapons.

Mr. Chairman,

The discourse about Islamic extremism, which has emerged as a long-standing global threat, and which has launched a wide-ranging assault on the achievements of human civilization, is not merely an academic or a theoretical exercise. Rather, the aim, here, is to find a viable and practical solution to safeguard humanity from this sinister phenomenon.

With the rise of ISIS and escalation of the crises in Iraq, Syria and Yemen, Islamic extremism has grown more vexing in recent months. But, for the Iranian people and Resistance this was not an unknown peril. Following the collapse of the Soviet Union and the 1991 Persian Gulf War, the Resistance warned that Islamic fundamentalism had emerged as the new global threat. Regrettably, this menace was not taken seriously.

Today, bloodied corpses of young school girls in Pakistan, kidnapping of innocent women and girls in Nigeria, beheading defenseless youth and forcible displacement of thousands of people in Iraq and Syria, appalling massacre of Sunnis in Iraq and their kidnapping, displacement, and forcible resettlement, terrorist attacks in Paris and Copenhagen, atrocious persistence and escalation of executions in Iran, coupled with the slaughter and imprisonment of religious minorities, have all deeply horrified the conscience of contemporary humanity.

Now, the people in the Middle East, Europe and elsewhere in the world are confronted with the greatest threat to the contemporary era: the challenge of extremism masquerading as Islam.

The question is: what is the main cause for the creation and rise of Islamic fundamentalism and where is its epicenter? Is the Shiite variant of extremism different from the Sunni one? Was the spread of such a malignant cancer inevitable? And finally, could this ominous phenomenon be defeated, and, if yes, what is the strategy to defeat it?

It is critical to answer these questions because they can serve as a guide to identify the solution and adopt the appropriate policies in dealing with this ominous phenomenon.

The main cause for the emergence and expansion of fundamentalism

The *velayat-e faqih* system that the founder of the Iranian regime, Khomeini, established after usurping the leadership of a popular revolution in Iran - made possible because the Shah's regime had suppressed the democratic and progressive movements and imprisoned their leadership - created for the first time in contemporary history a state that combined political power with "religious" authority: a medieval tyranny hiding behind the curtain of religion.

The ultimate and declared goal of fundamentalists has been to establish an Islamic Caliphate and enforce Sharia law by force. This objective is the common denominator and the focal point of all variants of Islamic fundamentalism whether Sunni or Shiite, which render their differences secondary in light of such commonality of purpose. Khomeini dubbed this as *"velayat-e motlaq-e faqih"* (absolute rule of the clergy), emphasizing that preserving "Islamic" rule took precedence over everything else.

This phenomenon is distinctly characterized by its aggressiveness and propensity for violence. It does not recognize any boundaries and its survival hinges on expansion. For this reason, from day one, the regime resorted to killings, torture and daily executions, coupled with stoning, eye-gouging and limb amputation, which have continued to this date. Simultaneously, it embarked on meddling in the affairs of other countries.

The *velayat-e faqih* system is incongruent with today's world, the people's needs and contemporary developments, and is incapable of resolving any political, social, economic or cultural problems in the 21st century. It therefore relies solely on naked violence, under the veneer of Islam, to prolong itself. The mullahs are intent on turning back the clock through sheer force, violence, and slaughter, which explains why they perpetrate countless atrocities.

Inside Iran, the mullahs eliminated women from political and social participation. Through discrimination, brutal crackdown, and imposition of mandatory veiling, they tried to intimidate and terrorize the citizenry. Under the banner of "cultural revolution" they shut down all universities for three years in order to set up educational entities totally in line with their own whims. They closed all newspapers that were critical of their policies and banned all dissident organizations, parties, and political entities.

Ethnic minorities were subjected to severe suppression and discrimination and religious minorities were brutally oppressed and deprived of their basic rights. This criminal conduct was quickly enshrined in the Constitution and institutionalized in the penal and civil codes, and continues today.

This is precisely the example, which both Sunni and Shiite extremists are following in other countries. This system of governance completely contradicts Islam and civilized norms. It is called an "Islamic Caliphate" by Sunni fundamentalists who adhere to the very same attributes and modus operandi. From a legal and religious standpoint, this system lacks the slightest capacity to change from within. The regime eliminates anyone challenging the absolute rule of the clergy.

As stipulated in its Constitution, the clerical regime formed the Revolutionary Guard Corps to protect the *velayat-e faqih* system and to expand it to other parts of the Islamic world.[2] It also created 75 different repressive agencies to leash and to suppress the public. To date, it has executed 120,000 political dissidents, ranging from 13-year-old girls to pregnant women and the elderly.[3]

Export of this medieval mindset, or, as Khomeini called it, export of revolution, is indispensable and inherent to the regime's modus operandi. The Iranian Resistance's leader Massoud Rajavi explained the principal theory behind the policy of exporting fundamentalism on several occasions. Incapable of guiding the enormous energy unleashed in the anti-monarchic revolution towards freedom, democracy and development, Khomeini squandered part of it in the war with Iraq and directed the rest outside the country under the pretext of 'exporting revolution,' he said.

---

[2] The Constitution of the Islamic Republic of Iran, Article 150. The Islamic Revolutionary Guards Corps, organized in the early days of the triumph of the Revolution, is to be maintained so that it may continue in its role of safeguarding the Revolution and its achievements.

[3] *Fallen for Freedom, 20,000 PMOI Martyrs – Partial List of 120,000 Victims of Political Executions in Iran under the Mullahs' Regime.* Compiled by the People's Mojahedin Organization of Iran on the Forty-first Anniversary of its Foundation – September 2006.

In reality, the existence of a tremendously young and restless society that overthrew the previous dictatorship has rendered this medieval regime permanently unstable, compelling it to export its backward ideology in order to put a lid on its internal crises.

In the Iranian regime's Constitution, the export of crisis, terrorism and fundamentalism has been codified in Articles 3, 11, and 154 under the guise of "relentless support for the *Mustazafan* (world's oppressed)" and "unity in the Islamic world." These are among the pillars of the regime's foreign policy.[4]

For Khomeini, exporting "Islamic revolution" to, and establishing a sister regime in Iraq was the first order of business. Doing so set the stage for a conflict that subsequently erupted when Iraq attacked Iran in 1980. By trying to dominate Iraq as early as in 1979 and subsequently perpetuating the unpatriotic Iran-Iraq war - with the mantra of "liberating Quds (Jerusalem) via Karbala - the regime sought to export its medieval ideology to the Islamic world. In contrast, the international community and the United Nations Security Council demanded an end to the war and called for a ceasefire. Khomeini had correctly realized that Iraq could be used as the springboard for encroaching upon the Arab and the Islamic world.

The enclosed map, published by the Revolutionary Guards Corps in the mid-1980s, exposes Khomeini's designs, in the midst of the Iran-Iraq War, to turn Iraq into a beachhead to dominate the Islamic world. Khomeini lost that war. But the international community's failure to grasp and understand the regime's nature and intentions and the resultant misguided policies in dealing with it, enabled Khomeini's successors to achieve that goal. Looking now, you can see that the regime has tried to encroach upon the very countries that it coveted to dominate in the early 1980s.

Khomeini had to accept defeat in the Iran-Iraq war in 1988. To prevent any social backlash he ordered the massacre of over 30,000 political prisoners in a matter of a few months. A majority of the victims belonged to PMOI/MEK, which ironically were Shiite Muslims.[5]

Today, the very officials responsible for the 1988 massacre occupy key positions in government agencies, including in Hassan Rouhani's cabinet and the regime's Judiciary.[6]

Parallel with the war with Iraq and particularly afterwards, the Iranian regime allocated an enormous budget to set up the so-called cultural and educational centers in different countries for the purpose of propagating its extremist ideology and recruiting adherents. In many places, including Lebanon, Palestinian territories, Syria, Iraq, and Yemen, it trained, funded, and armed both Shiite and Sunni terrorists.

---

[4] The Constitution of the Islamic Republic of Iran, Article 3, no. 16: Framing the foreign policy of the country on the basis of Islamic criteria, fraternal commitment to all Muslims, and unsparing support to the *Mustazafan* [abased] of the world Article 11: ...the government of the Islamic Republic of Iran has the duty of formulating its general policies with a view to cultivating the friendship and unity of all Muslim peoples, and it must constantly strive to bring about the political, economic, and cultural unity of the Islamic world. Article 154: while scrupulously refraining from all forms of interference in the internal affairs of other nations, it supports the just struggles of the *Mustazafan* (the abased) against the *Mustakberan* (oppressors) in every corner of the globe.
[5] Mojahed weekly publication, No. 427, February 9, 1999 — Containing the list of names and particulars of 3,208 massacred political prisoners.
[6] Mostafa Pourmohammadi, representative of the Intelligence Ministry in the Death Commission that was in charge of the massacre of political prisoners in 1988, is now the Minister of Justice in Rouhani's cabinet.

From the outset, the clerical regime tried to spread extremism by taking 52 Americans hostage for 444 days in 1979, blowing up the U.S. Marines barracks in Beirut in 1983, creating Hezbollah in Lebanon and the Supreme Council for Islamic Revolution in Iraq (SCIRI group) as well as a number of groups in other Muslim majority countries, and taking western citizens hostage in Lebanon.

This policy is not restricted to the past. In recent years, the policy of meddling in other countries' affairs has indeed intensified, taking on significantly deeper and broader dimensions. As such, fundamentalism acquired both a new form and broader dimensions, and grew by leveraging the unique cultural and historical standing of Iran, a country that has also been endowed with one of the world's largest oil and gas reserves.

In reality, Iran became the cultural capital of the Islamic world in the early decades after the advent of Islam so much so that any transformation or change in Iran has had an auxiliary impact on the world of Islam during the past 14 centuries. After Khomeini came to power, however, he placed Iran on a different path and transformed it into the epicenter of fundamentalism, crowning it as the godfather of extremists and terrorists in the Middle East.

It was only through the existence of the *velayat-e faqih* regime in Iran that Islamic fundamentalism morphed into a new global threat. Without the instrument of state power in a country like Iran, reactionary forces would not have mustered such potential and prospect to emerge as a destructive force.

This transformation would have been impossible without the central role of Iran, a vast, rich country situated in a strategic location and known for its unique influence in the Islamic world. Conversely, the collapse of this epicenter leads to the isolation and defeat of this ominous threat across the globe and renders it ineffectual.

Flawed dichotomy between Shiite and Sunni fundamentalism

Contrary to the realities underscored above, because ISIS and Sunni fundamentalist groups do not have a perceivable and clear link to the mullahs in Tehran and are hostile to one another in a number of areas, an artificial dichotomy has been assumed between Sunni and Shiite fundamentalists. Some policymakers and pundits therefore even view the Iranian regime as a potential partner in the fight against ISIS.

Meanwhile, Tehran's clerical rulers are expediently using both Sunni and Shiite extremist groups for the regime's own purposes. They direct Lebanon's Hezbollah and arm extremist Sunni groups in Arab countries. Over the past 20 years and at many important junctures, the Iranian regime provided enormous assistance to Sunni extremists like Al Qaeda. Since 2001, Tehran has provided safe haven to a number of Al Qaeda leaders, later facilitating their passage to Iraq, Syria, and other Muslim countries.

In February 2012, the regime's Supreme Leader Ali Khamenei emphasized, "The Islamic Revolution has a mandatory religious obligation to equally help both the Sunni and Shiite jihadists."[7]

On June 4, 2014, only three days before ISIS took over Mosul, Khamenei made a public speech in which he said: "Don't make a mistake. The enemy is America. *Takfiri* groups are just seditionists."[8] In the Iranian regime's lexicon, the loyal opposition is described as seditionist.

More importantly, if it were not for the Iranian regime's domination of Iraq, the sectarian policies of its puppet prime minister Nuri al-Maliki, and the massacre committed against the Sunni population in Iraq, and if it were not for the slaughter of 250,000 people in Syria by the Assad regime and the Iranian regime's Quds Force, ISIS would have never been able to find such a fertile breeding ground for its emergence and expansion.

In his will, Khomeini called for the overthrow of all existing governments in the Muslim world, followed by the eviction of their rulers, and establishment of "one Islamic State with free and independent republics."[9] The regime's current leader Khamenei declared himself the source of emulation for Shiites and the Supreme Leader for all Muslims. In other words, as it pertains to governance, Khamenei considers himself the ruler of all Muslims.[10]

---

[7] Khamenei's sermon at Tehran's Friday prayer, February 3, 2012: "We believe that Muslims, whether Sahfeii, Jaafari, Maleki, Hanbali or Zaidi, are all Islamic sects who are brothers and must have mutual respect for one another. They should have healthy, fraternal dialogues in Fiq'h, interpretation of words and history and work hand in hand to build a single, powerful, global Islamic Civilization of the Prophet Mohammad (S.A.W) in the contemporary time.

"Iran seeks not to make Arabs Persian or make Shiites out of other Muslims. Iran seeks to advocate the Quran and the tradition of the Prophet Mohammad (SAW) and his household (SAW) and revitalize the Islamic nation. For the Islamic Revolution there is a religious obligation and duty to assist the Sunni jihadists of the Hamas organizations as well as the Shiite jihadists of the Hezbollah on an equal level." (Iranian state-run News Network TV, February 3, 2012)

[8] Khamenei's speech at Khomeini's grave: "Today, some people in different parts of the world of Islam - which go by the name of Takfiri, Wahhabi and Salafi groups - are adopting bad and inappropriate measures against Iran, Shia Muslims and Shia Islam. But everyone should know that they are not the main enemies." (Iran's state-run News Network TV, June 4, 2014)

[9] Khomeini's last will, article F:

You, the meek of the world and Islamic countries and the world's Muslim, rise up and obtain your rights with empty hands. Do not fear the propaganda of the super powers and their subservient lackeys. Expel the criminal rulers who surrender your earnings to your enemies and the enemies of dear Islam

[10] Shob'heh website: Why is His Excellency, the leader, referred to as "the leader of the world's Muslims"?

    a. Not only is there a difference between a source of emulation and a ruler of an Islamic Government, but there is also a difference between a "decree" and a "fatwa". It is an obligation for the followers of a certain source of emulation to abide by his fatwa, whereas if a religious authority issues a "decree," all Shiites and even the authorities are obliged to follow it. (Like the decree issued by Mirza Shirazi boycotting tobacco)

    b. Therefore, under the rule of a religious authority, it is an obligation to abide by his governmental orders. Therefore, he is their Imam and their leader.

    c. Today, there are two billion Muslims in the world. Nearly 500 million of them are Shiites. Therefore, in light of the fact that it is an obligation for all Muslims to follow the orders of "the Guardian of all Muslims" or "the Velayat-e Faqih" (absolute clerical rule), it is clear that he is the leader of all Muslims around the world.

The terrorist Quds Force, formed a quarter of a century ago, is the instrument for exporting extremism to not only Shiite but also to Sunni communities.

Theoretically speaking, fundamentalism represents a perverted view of Islam. What is presented under the banner of these two aberrations in the Islamic faith, are in essence one and the same thing. Both emphasize misogyny and religious discrimination. Both, impose religion and beliefs through the use of force, contrary to Quranic verses; both rely on the laws of past millennia called Sharia to enforce the most violent and inhumane forms of punishment; both pursue a reactionary caliphate, which translates into the cruel rule of an individual tyrant. One calls it the *velayat-e motlaq-e faqih* (the absolute rule of clergy) while the other refers to it as a Caliph. Of course, three decades ago, Khomeini explicitly said in a public speech that "We want a Caliph who would amputate limbs, flog and stone to death."[11]

Shiite fundamentalists, however, are more dangerous than their Sunni counterparts because they rely on a regional power, namely the religious dictatorship ruling Iran. Look at the situation in Iraq and what is happening there on a daily basis. The mullahs' so-called Shiite militias act more viciously than their Sunni equivalents, such as ISIS. In the long run, they pose a much greater threat than their Sunni brethren to Iraq's independent existence and regional peace, security, and stability. With the help of these militias, the mullahs have turned four Arab countries into theaters of their terrorism and destruction.

The militia groups in Iraq, the Hezbollah in Lebanon, and the Houthis in Yemen are under total control and backing of the mullahs' Revolutionary Guards Corps (IRGC) and Khamenei. The Iranian regime is Bashar Assad's main patron and the primary factor for keeping him in power is Syria. In September 2014, a member of mullahs' parliament (Majlis) said, "Currently, three Arab capitals are in the hands of Iran, and Sana'a will be the fourth... We seek the unification of Islamic countries."[12]

A Friday prayer leader added that the borders of the Islamic Republic had reached Yemen.[13] A number of the highest ranking regime officials, including Khamenei's senior advisor, explicitly and publicly called Syria an Iranian province.[14]

In short, the regime ruling Iran is the axis of Islamic fundamentalism in terms of ideology, policies, money, weapons, and logistical support. Beyond any form of concrete political or financial link between these sorts of groups and Tehran, the determining factor is the presence of a fundamentalist regime in power in Iran (*the velayat-e faqih*), which presents a model and inspires the formation of all fundamentalist groups and cells. In the absence of

---

[11] Khomeini's speech on the anniversary of the birth of the Prophet of Islam In 1982.

[12] A Majlis (parliament) deputy said on September 18, 2014: Currently, there are three Arab capitals in the hands of Iran and Sana'a [in Yemen] will the fourth capital...We are seeking to integrate all Islamic countries."

[13] Khamenei's representative and the Friday prayer leader of Zanjan province said: The boundaries of the Islamic Republic are in Yemen and attacking Yemen is the same as attacking the Islamic Republic." IRNA, state-run news agency, April 17, 2015.

[14] Mullah Mehdi Ta'eb, Khamenei's chief advisor: "Syria is the 35th province of the country and a strategic province for us." Fars News Agency, February 14, 2013.

such a regime, there would be no intellectual, ideological, or political space, or a central base and dependable epicenter for the emergence and growth of such groups.

As long as the Tehran regime is not replaced by a democratic, tolerant, and pluralist government, the problem of Islamic fundamentalism will persist regardless of any military and security confrontation, every time emerging in different variations.

The nuclear bomb in the policy of export of fundamentalism and terrorism

Nuclear weapons serve both to guarantee the survival of the Iranian regime and pave the way for exporting fundamentalism.

The clerical regime's former president and current head of the Expediency Council Ali-Akbar Hashemi Rafsanjani, boasted in the early 1990s, "If we acquire nuclear weapons, who could prevent the export of the revolution to Islamic countries?"

Khamenei's fatwa about nuclear weapons being *haram* (forbidden) is a hoax. Many years ago, Khomeini reminded Khamenei that the *vali-e faqih* (supreme ruler) has the power to unilaterally abrogate his religious commitments to the citizenry if that were to serve the interests of the state.

By acquiring a nuclear bomb, the Iranian regime seeks to upend the regional balance of power and subsequently exert its hegemony over the whole region. To be sure, a nuclear-armed or nuclear threshold regime in Iran will propel an arms race across the region; but this is only the lesser consequence. The primary fallout would be the Iranian regime's domination of the political, economic, and military disposition of the region and of many Muslim countries.

It would be a fatal mistake to believe that silence and accommodation vis-à-vis the regime's onslaught throughout the region would help advance the nuclear talks. Tehran is intimating this approach in different ways and, of course, has so far taken full advantage of it to advance its designs both regarding its nuclear projects and meddling in the region. Firmness in dealing with the regime will force it to retreat. Giving concessions to it, on the other hand, will embolden it to be more aggressive.

Nuclear program: National pride or spreading fundamentalism in the region?

To describe the mullahs' nuclear weapons program as a source of "national pride" is an affront to the Iranian people who believe otherwise. Using this pretext to offer concessions to the clerics is therefore unacceptable. The mullahs seek to obtain nuclear weapons to preserve their regime and export their reactionary mindset to the region, both of which are contrary to the interests and yearnings of the Iranian people.

Iran does not need nuclear energy because it does not make economic sense! The clerical regime has invested hundreds of billions of dollars in this program while lack of sufficient investment in the oil industry has left the country without adequate refineries, compelling it to import gasoline from abroad. This is tantamount to a disaster.[15]

Our 36-year experience has made it palpably clear that the mullahs only understand the language of firmness and power. Those who reject a nuclear-armed theocracy and stand with the Iranian people must refrain from appeasing and offering concessions to a murderous religious dictatorship, which is, at the same time the central banker of terrorism and the world record holder in per capita execution of its citizens. The world community must recognize the rights of the Iranian people to fight for freedom. Accordingly, on behalf of the Iranian people's Resistance, I emphasize:

1. The regime's nuclear program runs counter to the national interests of the Iranian people, who strongly opposed it. In contrast to the mullahs' regime, we seek a democratic, non-nuclear Iran. Out of 80 million Iranians no fewer than 50 million live below the poverty line;

2. Acquiring a nuclear arsenal, abusing human rights, and exporting fundamentalism and terrorism are indispensable features of the ruling theocracy. Upholding human rights in Iran and forcing the regime to withdraw from Iraq, Syria, Lebanon, Yemen, and Afghanistan offer a real yardstick to ascertain whether or not the regime has abandoned its nuclear weapons program. Anything short, however camouflaged or presented, amounts to self-delusion and acquiesces to the catastrophe of a nuclear-armed theocracy;

3. Adding six or nine months to the nuclear breakout time while dealing with a regime that has been engaged in a three-decade game of hide and cheat does not provide a solution. The only guarantee to secure the world from the threat of a nuclear disaster is to fully implement six Security Council resolutions on Iran's nuclear program, completely halt enrichment, and compel the regime to shut down its nuclear sites as well as WMD and missile programs;

4. Snap inspections anytime, anywhere, of all suspect sites, military or otherwise, are critical in preventing the mullahs from obtaining the bomb;

5. The Iranian regime must be obliged to provide satisfactory answers on the possible military dimensions (PMD) of its nuclear projects (before a final agreement is reached), make available its nuclear experts and documents, and unveil networks involved in smuggling nuclear equipment and material into Iran;

6. The notion of snapping back the sanctions in the event Tehran violates its commitments or cheats is neither practical nor feasible. None of the sanctions should

---

[15] Given the increase in population and growing demand for cars on a per capita basis, Iran is in need of gasoline and is one of the biggest importers of fuel.

Name of refinery	daily production capacity	daily production of gas (liter/day)
Abadan	9138	1291
Tehran	1700	1348
Kermanshah	1137	1350
Shiraz	1903	1352
Lavan	987	1355
Tabriz	2884	1327
Isfahan	7568	1357
Arak	4760	1372
Bandar Abbas	13000	1376

(BBC, August 30, 2011)

be lifted before an agreement has been signed that effectively and definitively denies the mullahs the bomb. Otherwise, the regime will spend billions of unfrozen assets to buy weapons including advanced missiles from Russia.

The spread of Islamic fundamentalism was not inevitable

The perceived power of Islamic fundamentalism in general and its epicenter in Tehran in particular, lies neither in its capacity nor its potential to achieve dominance; but is the consequence of the absence of a timely response to this phenomenon. Lack of such a timely response is the by-product of the fact that Islamic fundamentalism has not been properly grasped or understood, something that has led to the adoption of misguided policies. Specifically:

1. Ignoring the threat of Islamic fundamentalism following the collapse of the Soviet Union and the Persian Gulf war in 1991;
2. Overlooking that post-9/11 developments in the region overshadowed the role of the epicenter of fundamentalism, i.e., the Iranian regime, giving it the opportunity to implement its plans for spreading extremism in the region;
3. Failing to thwart Tehran's increasing meddling in Iraq after 2003, which led to the gradual hand-over of Iraq to the mullahs. The regime thus received on a silver platter the very prize it could not win during eight years of war with Iraq in the 1980s, despite one million dead, two million wounded and disabled on the Iranian side alone, one trillion dollars in economic damage, and destruction of 3,000 cities and villages.
   The mullahs' domination of Iraq, especially under al-Maliki, was the outcome of one of the greatest geopolitical blunders after World War II. It had dire implications for the whole region, including the rise of ISIS and the crises in Syria and Yemen.

4. Disarming and interning the PMOI/MEK (the main Iranian opposition and the only organized, anti-fundamentalist Muslim movement), its subsequent handover to Maliki's puppet regime as well as silence and inaction vis-à-vis repeated attacks on its members in Iraq.

   In addition, the PMOI/MEK and the National Council of Resistance of Iran, (a coalition of democratic forces seeking regime change in Iran) were blacklisted for 15 years, effectively restraining their enormous wherewithal and wasting their resources, which could have otherwise been utilized to effectuate change in Iran. These actions were the best signals to Tehran to continue its efforts to acquire the bomb and export terrorism and fundamentalism with impunity and without having to worry about its popular and legitimate opposition.

A firm policy by the West and support for the Iranian people's aspirations for change and a different approach to the Resistance movement that is the antithesis to the mullahs' fundamentalism would have prevented the spread of extremism and terrorism masquerading as Islam.

The formation of a regional coalition and the launching of Operation Decisive Storm to end the occupation of Yemen by the Iranian regime's proxies was the first such initiative in the past 25 years that acted as an obstacle to the regime's escalating regional meddling.

Time has come to learn from past experience. Since 1993, the Iranian Resistance has been warning about the threat of fundamentalism emanating from the Iranian regime. And since 2003, we have consistently revealed the regime's interference in Iraq. Unfortunately, those warnings have not been heeded. Today, I reiterate that the mullahs are not part of the solution; they are indeed part of the problem. We must stand up to Tehran's meddling in Iraq. Under no circumstances should the Iraqi militias affiliated with the Iranian regime be legitimized. The solution is to evict the Iranian regime from Iraq.

Bargaining for the maximum to preserve the minimum

The mullahs need to export fundamentalism, war, and terror under the banner of Islam beyond Iranian borders to preserve their power in Tehran. One of the essential attributes of fundamentalism is that it can only survive by being on the offensive. Confining the Iranian regime within its own borders and compelling it to abandon its nuclear projects lay bare its real and underlying weaknesses and expedites its downfall.

Khamenei and other regime officials have repeatedly attested to this reality: one step backward is tantamount to retreating all the way back to the overthrow of the state. In December 2014, the Secretary of the regime's Supreme National Security Council, Ali Shamkhani, touched on this point after the killing of one of the most senior commanders of the Quds Force in Iraq. Speaking at his funeral, Shamkhani said, "Those who are sick rumormongers ask us why we interfere in Iraq or Syria. The answer to this question is clear. If [our commanders] do not sacrifice their blood in Iraq, then our blood will be shed in Tehran, Azerbaijan, Shiraz, and Isfahan." Shamkhani emphasized: "To avoid having our blood spilled in Tehran, we must sacrifice our blood in Iraq and defend it." [16]

The 2009 uprising demonstrated that the people of Iran, especially youths and women, are looking for the opportunity to bring fundamental change to Iran. While the Sunni extremists recruit young people in Arab countries and even in some European capitals, in Iran, young people are engaged in a fierce battle against the ruling theocracy. For the past 36 years, the people of Iran have experienced this ominous phenomenon in all its political, social, and economic spheres. An ocean of blood lies between them and the ruling regime.

The reason is that an organized and cohesive force that adheres to Islam, the PMOI/MEK, promoted in Iranian society a culture of tolerance and belief in freedom. It challenged, with all its might, the violent extremist interpretations of Islam and offered an anti-fundamentalist cultural alternative to Iranian society.

Therefore, as the regime becomes weaker and more isolated inside the country it senses a greater need for aggression beyond its borders. Mindful that Islamic fundamentalism has failed in Iran and is detested by the Iranian people, the mullahs have stepped up domestic repression and resorted to terrorism and warmongering as never before in order to preserve

---

[16] Ali Shamkhani, secretary of the Supreme Security Council: "There are sick people who spread rumors these days, asking about the connection between Samara [in Iraq] and Hamid Taqavi. They ask what do we have to do with Iraq and Syria? The answer to this question is clear. If the likes of Taqavi do not give their blood in Samara, then we would have our blood shed in Sistan, Azerbaijan, Shiraz and Isfahan." Fars News Agency, December 29, 2014.

their theocracy, misogyny, religious discrimination, or, in a nutshell, maintain their fragile grip on power.

Recall that in the final year of the Second World War, even as the Nazis continued to pose the greatest threat to humanity, they was incapable of preventing the inevitable cracks forming within their rotting core, which rapidly brought its downfall.

The need for a cultural and religious response to fundamentalism

An accurate assessment of developments in recent years leads to a very important conclusion that Islamic fundamentalism and extremism are vulnerable and can therefore be defeated. To do so, there is need for a firm comprehensive policy and also a focus on the epicenter, i.e., the regime in Tehran. But reinforcing and increasing intelligence gathering capabilities and intensifying military operations would in and of themselves be insufficient.

A political, religious, and cultural antidote is required to uproot this cancerous tumor permanently. In absence of an alternative interpretation of Islam – which would in fact represent the true spirit of Islam, one that would espouse tolerance, liberty, and freedom of choice for the people, extremist ringleaders will portray the war against fundamentalism as a fight against Islam itself. By doing so, they will then create the most important source of nourishment for this ominous phenomenon. We must demarcate between the true Islam and this rigid reactionary mindset, while exposing and drying up the resources for demagoguery and exploitation of Islam by fundamentalists, especially the Iranian regime. This will not be an easy task and will not come to fruition merely through charming rhetoric.

Fortunately for Iran, the PMOI/MEK is largest political opposition organization and offers a cultural and ideological alternative to Islamic fundamentalism.

Throughout its fifty-year-long history, the PMOI/MEK has posed a political and cultural challenge to Islamic dogmatism. It believes that fundamentalists are ironically the greatest enemies of Islam itself, that their views and conduct have nothing to do with genuine Islam and the Quran and that Islam must be reclaimed.

This organization began to engage in an extensive cultural, social, and political campaign after the fall of the Shah. It was active among the youth in high schools and universities, among women and workers, as well as a wide array of other social sectors and worked to expose the medieval, backward, and anti-democratic nature of Khomeini and his band of clerics. It also introduced democratic Islam. In the course of just 2.5 years, it succeeded in educating a large segment of Iranian society, recruiting them away from the ruling mullahs, before the regime eliminated all peaceful avenues of political activity.

During the first Iranian presidential elections, Massoud Rajavi was the PMOI's candidate, and received widespread support from all social sectors thanks to his adherence to a platform that focused on political and social freedoms that was diametrically opposed to the culture of the Islamic fundamentalism. Khomeini was so gravely concerned that a majority would cast their ballots to elect Rajavi that he vetoed his candidacy. According to official counts, Mr. Rajavi received over half a million votes in Tehran during the first parliamentary elections, despite massive electoral fraud.[17]

Democratic Islam; Response to Islamic Fundamentalism

The Islam to which we adhere is a democratic Islam.

In contrast, the declared objective of Islamic fundamentalism is enforcing Sharia law by force. This goal is the common denominator between the *velayat-e faqih* regime in Iran and Islamic Caliphate of ISIS.

As a Muslim, I declare:

Anything enforced by force and compulsion is not Islam. Neither religion, nor prayer, nor hijab can be enforced through force. As the Holy Quran says, "There is no compulsion in religion."[18]

Freedom is the underlying message of Islam. As the Quran says, Islam has come to free the people from the shackles, not to impose Sharia law.[19]

What fundamentalists present as Sharia law has nothing to do with Islam; it is contrary to the teachings of Islam. The fundamentalists' Sharia law is either self-invented or belongs to the past millennia and only serves them to gain or preserve power. Anything that enchains human beings and deprives them of freedom, choice, and dignity contradicts Islam.

Islam is the religion of compassion and freedom. God Almighty designated the Prophet to be mercy to the worlds.[20]

Islam considers sovereignty to be the greatest right bestowed upon the people. It condemns dictatorship in any form or under any banner. Islam is based on consultation, freedom of choice, expression, and belief.[21]

According to the Quran, people of all races, creeds and genders are equal. Islam defends and encourages human progress and achievements. Consistent with this teaching, the PMOI/MEK has over the past 36 years been advocating democracy, pluralism, and separation of religion and state.

Islam profoundly respects human rights and views the killing of even one man as killing of all of humanity.[22] Islam respects all religions. The Quran insists that there are no differences between prophets.[23]

---

[17] The Election Results, *Ettela'at* Newspaper, 13 April 1980.

[18] The Holy Quran, Chapter 2, *Baqarah* (Cow), verse 256.

[19] The Holy Quran, Chapter 7, *Al-A'raf* (The Heights), verse 157.

[20] The Holy Quran, Chapter 21, *Al-Anbya* (The Prophets), verse 107.

[21] The Holy Quran, Chapter 42, *Ash-Shura* (The Consultation), verse 38; Chapter 3, *Ali Imran* (Family of Imran), verse 159.

[22] The Holy Quran, Chapter 5, *Al-Maidah* (The Table Spread), verse 32.

[23] The Holy Quran, Chapter 2, *Baqarah* (Cow), verse 285.

This message can defeat Islamic fundamentalism in its most important ideological epicenter. For this reason, democratic and tolerant Islam, which is the true Islam not distorted by the mullahs, is the antithesis to fundamentalism.

By adhering to this mindset, the PMOI/MEK plays a decisive role in the cultural and intellectual defeat of the clerical regime and its isolation within Iran as the godfather of Islamic fundamentalism.

This movement, owing both to its enduring campaign against the religious fascism ruling Iran and paying the enormous cost of this struggle, is uniquely qualified to confront Islamic fundamentalism.

Strategy to overcome fundamentalism

With the coming to power of the mullahs in Iran, Islamic extremism emerged as a threat to peace and security. It spread extensively after 2003 when the Iranian regime began to dominate Iraq. So long as the mullahs remain in power in Iran, the crisis will continue in one way or the other. Thus, the ultimate solution is to overthrow the Iranian regime, which can only be achieved by the people of Iran and Iranian Resistance. However, in order to prevent further deepening of the crisis and putting an end to this catastrophe, the international community needs to take the following steps.

1. Take practical measures to evict the Iranian regime from Iraq. Only then will fundamentalism begin to retreat, because this is precisely where it has expanded. The Quds Force, the Shiite militias, and other proxies of the Iranian regime who have penetrated deep into the political, military, security, and economic fabric of Iraq during the eight years of Maliki, must be removed from power structures. It would be a big mistake to seek the help of these Shiite militias in confronting ISIS. The only appropriate response to ISIS is to trust, empower, and arm the Sunnis and engage them in power sharing in a realistic and meaningful way.

2. Help the people of Syria overthrow Bashar Assad and move toward democracy. The crimes of the Assad regime, which remains in power with the backing of Tehran and the IRGC, is the greatest cause of Sunni extremists' success in recruiting volunteers. Had there been a proper response to the Assad regime's shocking chemical attack in a Damascus suburb, ISIS would have certainly not been so powerful today. The crimes of the Iranian regime and Bashar Assad in Syria, which have left hundreds of thousands dead and more than 10 million people homeless, are the greatest cause of rage and hatred among Sunni Muslims.

3. Instead of appeasing the heart of fundamentalism and terrorism, i.e., the mullahs' regime, the Iranian people's desire and will to overthrow the clerical regime must be recognized. Silence vis-à-vis blatant and systematic abuse of human rights and escalating trend of mass executions in Iran provide the greatest encouragement to extremists.

A very important part of this approach would be to uphold the rights and guarantee the protection of Camp Liberty residents. Far beyond a humanitarian issue and violation of repeated written commitments by the U.S. and the U.N., the predicament of PMOI/MEK members in Iraq since 2003 has only benefited the Iranian regime and paved the way for expansion of extremism.

As 5.2 million Iraqis declared in a statement in 2006, the PMOI/MEK is the most significant political and cultural bulwark against the spread and penetration of fundamentalism. After the U.S. handed over the protection of Camp Ashraf residents to Iran's puppet regime in Iraq, 116 of residents were killed in six lethal attacks by Iraqi Security Forces. Twenty-five more lost their lives due to an inhumane medical blockade and lack of timely access to medical care. Seven were also taken hostage in 2013, whose fate and whereabouts remain unknown.

4. There must be an emphasis on a democratic and tolerant interpretation of Islam to challenge fundamentalist interpretations whether Shiite or Sunni variants.

5. A decisive policy vis-à-vis the Iranian regime's nuclear program is vital to block its pathways to the bomb. This would play an important role in eliminating fundamentalism in the region because it would weaken its epicenter and limit the scope of its aggression.

Mr. Chairman,
Distinguished representatives,

Today, the clerical regime is engulfed in deep crisis at home. The people of Iran reject this totalitarian theocracy. They long for freedom, democracy, and regime change.

The Iranian regime is also facing a crippling economic crisis. Corruption has permeated the entire structure of the regime. Official figures say 12 million people go hungry in Iran.[24] Iran has one of the highest inflation rates and the unemployment rate stands at no less than 40 percent.[25] Nevertheless, Rouhani increased the IRGC budget by 50 percent.[26]

Despite a state of absolute repression, protests are spreading by the day. On April 15, one million Iranian teachers staged a nationwide protest in 27 out of 31 provinces. Workers' protests and strikes are also escalating every day.[27]

The proponents of "moderation" within the Iranian regime, such as Rouhani, share the views of other factions regarding the regime's redlines and totalitarian rule of the Supreme Leader. They are partners in domestic repression and exporting terrorism. Contrary to claims by the regime's appeasers, not only are they not a force for change but serve to

---

[24] Ali Rabii, Minister of Cooperation, Labor and Social Affairs – Mehr News Agency, December 5, 2014.
[25] Iranian Economy Website – November 18, 2014.
[26] Iranian Fiscal Year Budget 1394 (March 2015 – March 2016) – Eghtesad News, January 7, 2015.
[27] The Associated Press. April 16, 2015: "Iran's semi-official ILNA news agency says thousands of teachers have staged nationwide protests demanding higher wages. The report says peaceful protests were held Thursday in several cities, including the capital, Tehran. It says the teachers gathered in silence in front of provincial Education Ministry buildings. In Tehran, hundreds of teachers gathered in front of parliament. The protesters carried placards in which they asked for higher wages and demanded the release of teachers allegedly detained in similar protests last month."

prolong the *velayat-e faqih* regime. Comparing them with the opposition to other autocratic regimes is misguided. As long as this regime remains in power, Islamic fundamentalism will persist as the main global threat.

The National Council of Resistance of Iran (NCRI) is a coalition comprised of 500 members, half of whom are women. It consists of democratic forces who seek to overthrow the regime in its entirety and establish a pluralist and secular republic. The NCRI has been waging a resistance against the Iranian regime for 34 years. In addition to a broad-base of support at home, it has gained extensive international recognition and is supported by a wide spectrum of political tendencies in Europe, the United States and Arab and Muslim countries.

According to the NCRI's constitution, a provisional government will be formed for an interim period of only six months after the overthrow of the clerical regime to facilitate the transfer of sovereignty to the people of Iran. It is tasked with holding a free and fair election with international observers, to elect a National Legislative and Constituent Assembly, which will draft a new constitution and run the country's affairs until the constitution of the new republic is ratified.

Consistent with its constitution and ratifications, the NCRI is committed to the Universal Declaration of Human Rights, the International Covenant on Civil and Political Rights, and other relevant international conventions. It is also committed to separation of religion and state and gender equality. I have outlined the Iranian Resistance's platform for future of Iran in the following 10-point platform:[28]

1. In our view, the ballot box is the only criterion for legitimacy. Accordingly, we seek a republic based on universal suffrage.
2. We want a pluralist system, freedom of parties and assembly. We respect all individual freedoms. We underscore complete freedom of expression and of the media and unconditional access by all to the Internet.
3. We are committed to the abolition of death penalty.
4. We are committed to separation of Religion and State. Any form of discrimination against the followers of any religion and denomination will be prohibited.
5. We believe in complete gender equality in political, social, and economic arenas. We are also committed to equal participation of women in political leadership. Any form of discrimination against women will be abolished. Women will enjoy the right to select their own clothing and will be free to make their own choices regarding marriage, divorce, education, and employment.
6. We believe in the rule of law and justice. We want to set up a modern judicial system based on the principles of presumption of innocence, the right to defense, effective judicial protection, and the right to be tried in a public court. We also seek the total independence of judges. Sharia law will be abolished.
7. We are committed to the Universal Declaration of Human Rights and international covenants and conventions, including the International Covenant on Civil and Political Rights, the Convention against Torture, and the Convention on the Elimination of all Forms of Discrimination against Women. We are committed to the

---

[28] Maryam Rajavi's vision for the future of Iran – June 22, 2013. Available at: http://www.maryam-rajavi.com/en/index.php?option=com_content&view=article&id=1452&Itemid=592

equality of all ethnicities. We underscore the plan for the autonomy of Iranian Kurdistan and hold that the language and culture of our compatriots, from whatever ethnicity, are among our nation's precious human resources and must be protected and celebrated in tomorrow's Iran.

8. We recognize private property, private investment, and the market economy. All Iranian people must enjoy equal opportunity in employment and in business ventures. We will protect and revitalize the environment.

9. Our foreign policy will be based on peaceful coexistence, international and regional peace and cooperation, as well as respect for the United Nations Charter.

10. We want a non-nuclear Iran, free of weapons of mass destruction.

Let me conclude my remarks by quoting one of the pioneers of the American civil rights movement, the Reverend Martin Luther King, Jr.: "The arch of the moral universe is long, but it bends towards justice." Our movement has existed before the Iranian Revolution and we have faith that with your help we can move the arch of the moral universe more quickly because our cause is just.

Thank you all very much.

Mr. POE. Thank you, Madam Rajavi.

We will have questions for you momentarily. But first, we will hear from Dr. Phares, and for the record both your testimony and Ms. Rajavi's testimony will be made a part of the record and you can summarize your testimony, Dr. Phares.

STATEMENT OF WALID PHARES, PH.D., CO-SECRETARY GENERAL, TRANSATLANTIC PARLIAMENTARY GROUP ON COUNTERTERRORISM

Mr. PHARES. Mr. Chairman, thank you very much for the invitation. I would like to thank also the ranking member and the members of the committee for organizing this very important strategic seminar hearing on ISIS—defining the enemy.

My testimony has the title "Identifying the Jihadi Ideology and Providing Alternative Strategies to Defeat ISIS," which I believe is the heart of the discussion on this panel.

For the sake of summary, I would like to go over the major principles I began with, the four points I would like to raise.

Point number one is about the ideology displayed by the Islamic State, its roots, its evolution and ultimately its final goals, and the question I raise: Are we dealing with a new ideology?

Is ISIS producing a new ideology, or is it an ideology that has been around through various organizations, various movements and now has reached a mutation that is allowing ISIS to win and win further?

Point two I am going to raise is about what happens if ISIS is unchecked. If the current situation of status quo, which I call a moving status quo—take a few villages, they take back a few villages despite the destruction of their military machine—if that situation continues, what should we be expecting in Iraq—in Iraq and Syria, in the region and beyond? And maybe beyond is in our homelands, including the United States and across the Atlantic.

Three—there is a current geopolitical problem or a series of problems in the confrontation with ISIS nowadays as we speak. I would like to offer a very short identification of what these two problems are—why we are obstructed, why we are not ending ISIS, as many in this House and the Senate and European Parliament have been asking.

And last, what can the United States and its allies do or actually, I would say, should do, to defeat ISIS and the movements behind ISIS—because ISIS is just a stage in a movement that began before and will continue later.

In my past 30 years of research, in six books focusing on future jihad and the evolution of this war of ideas, I have made the case that what we are dealing with, particularly since 9/11—and the 9/11 Commission has been very clear on this—we are dealing with an ideology that is producing a movement, not a movement that is producing the ideology.

Hence, I have recommended that the United States, to the past administration and this administration and future administrations, actually engage in a battle that we have not engaged in, which is to respond to the ideology, to actually mobilize those forces and civil societies that can respond to this ideology.

And after doing this we can encourage the societies that could be and would be freed from ISIS to form an intellectual resistance to stop the return of ISIS. Remember, dear members, that we were in Iraq. We left Iraq.

There was an Iraqi army. That Iraqi army was in the Sunni areas. So the maximum that our hopes would be right now would be for the same forces to go into the same regions, to defeat ISIS.

We have defeated al-Qaeda before. So there is a constant phenomenon that keeps bringing the jihadists back, not just to Iraq this time, but to Syria and as far as Libya and Yemen and north Nigeria.

I have suggested in my research that, number one, we need to identify the ideology but, number two, we need to have a coalition with forces that are willing to push back against the ideology.

One cannot win a war of ideas from an American perspective against the whole world. We need to have allies, and the most important ally should be in the region. The problem has been, in the past, that we have ignored them.

We have partnered with many forces, but I assume and I will make the case that we have partnered with the wrong persons, with the wrong forces.

Partnering, for example, with the Muslim Brotherhood. Even though this is based on the notion that moderate Islamists can be a wall against extremist Islamists—that is what we have heard from Washington over the past years—we forget one thing: That we do not control what happens.

If we support the moderate Islamists without making sure that they are vetted, that they will move against the jihadists, what will happen? And it already happened in Syria; when we supported moderate Islamists, they became al-Nusra and from al-Nusra they ended up becoming ISIS.

So we need to have a better, not just vetting system, but a better system of ideas upon which we can develop the strategy.

Last but not least, in my last book, ''The Lost Spring,'' I urged the administration and, of course, Congress to act faster before the catastrophes hit—that was last March—before ISIS takes over half of Syria and one-third of Iraq, before ISIS lands in Benghazi and Derna, before the Houthi pro-Iranian militias expand. All of this happened since last June.

If you look at the map—the historical map of these events, most of the explosions that we are dealing with happened over the past 9 months.

On the ideological level, it is clear that this group, ISIS, has not invented new ideas. The success of ISIS is that it has made into reality all the dreams of the previous ideologies and previous jihadists.

What is ISIS in Iraq and Syria? It is the dream of bin Laden. He spoke about it—killing infidels: Every single jihadist since the '20s has been talking about it.

The major difference is that this Daesh, ISIS or ISIL has been able to do it because of their strength, because of the chaos in the region but, I would add, because of our policies, which were not preemptive enough nor formed the right coalitions at the right time.

Second, if not checked, ISIS is projected to increase its control of the Sunni areas where they are. But that control is not going to be only military.

My concern and the concern of many of my colleagues who have been looking at what this organization is doing, number one: They are drafting.

So we are not just talking about individuals who have been in al-Qaeda and other places and now adhering to ISIS. They are going into cities and towns and drafting. So their numbers are supposed to grow.

My greater concern, dear members, is that they are now schooling. They are doing in Iraq and in Syria what the Taliban did two decades ago in parts of Afghanistan and in Pakistan.

They are creating already the next generation, and this is not something secret. We don't even need intelligence to know that. It is on YouTube.

We see those kids aged between eight and 12 being schooled into ideological madrassas and hence my first conclusion. Even if we take back Mosul, if we take back Tikrit, if we take back Raqqa in Syria or others would do, my concern is that the next generation is being worked on right now. So we need to have a strategy with regard the ideological confrontation.

Third, on the geopolitical problems that we are facing in fighting ISIS today I would identify two major obstructions. One, definitely, and it responds to my concern: We don't have a war of ideas.

I have reviewed every single piece of what we call in Washington a strategic communications campaign, a de-radicalization campaign. I will be more than happy to expand on that when and if needed.

We are not winning on the ideological level. An argument such the one discussed earlier that a jihadi becomes jihadi because there is no job—and I am not talking about the politics of it, I am talking about the academic dimension of it—that argument is not true.

It has been debunked in the Middle East. When you talk to intellectuals in Egypt and Libya and Tunisia and other parts of the Middle East, they do not adopt this argument.

A jihadi becomes a jihadi simply because of indoctrination, and the evidence is if you have 1 million individuals in any country in the Middle East that are jobless, why would 500 of these 1 million choose to become jihadi? What is the difference?

Why wouldn't the 1 million become jihadists? It is the same frustration. The others would choose to become revolutionaries, reformers, do demonstrations, find a job. They would choose many other options.

Science and research have told us those who have shifted to become jihadists, even if they are under duress sociologically, have been indoctrinated before.

There is a chip that was put in their mind by different ways that allowed them to take the argumentation of we are now jihadists. And, by the way, dear members, the jihadists themselves never use the socioeconomic element.

They would never say, "I didn't find a job or I was frustrated, therefore I became." They didn't even use the norm of, "We are against the richer people."

Their concern is caliphate or no caliphate. Their concern is to win that battle on the ground or not.

[The prepared statement of Mr. Phares follows:]

Walid Phares, Ph.D.
Co-Secretary General
Transatlantic Parliamentary Group on Counterterrorism

Testimony for the Hearing on
"ISIS: Defining the Enemy"

Testimony Title:

"Identifying the Jihadi Ideology and Alternative Strategies to Defeat IS"

House Committee on Foreign Affairs
Subcommittee on Terrorism, Nonproliferation, and Trade

April 29, 2015

Introduction: ISIS a strategic threat and a genocidal terror movement

In our assessment, based on thirty years of studying, monitoring, publishing and teaching about the global Jihadist movement, the so-called Islamic State, known as Daesh, ISIS or ISIL, which describes itself as a Caliphate and controls large swaths of land between Mosul in Iraq and Reqqa in Syria, this organization is simultaneously a strategic threat to the region and to the world and a genocidal terror movement. In this short testimony, I wish to share with the members of the panel and with the U.S. House in general, four major findings on this Jihadi menace:
1. The ideology displayed by the Islamic State (IS), its roots, its evolution and ultimately its final goals;
2. The current and future geopolitical consequences, of an unchecked IS;
3. The current geopolitical problems in fighting IS;
4. What the United States and its allies can and should do to defeat IS and the movement in general.

Back in 2005, ten years ago, I published a book titled *Future Jihad: Terrorist Strategies against America and the West* in which I projected the rise of a mutant and urban Jihadist movement which would take multiple forms, adopt different names, and survive the fall of organizations allowing the global movement to continue as long as it was fed by generations of recruits, themselves produced by an ideological factory. I had argued then, and continue to underline a decade later, that as long as the ideological factory is operational, there will be Jihadi movements, from al Qaeda to IS, as well as post-ISIS organizations, even if a ground offensive in Iraq and Syria dismantles the militia's strongholds.

In 2008, I published a book titled *The Confrontation: Winning the War against Future Jihad* in which I suggested two strategies to defeat these movements. One strategy was to engage in a war of ideas by identifying the terror ideology, and the second included forming the right coalitions, based on strategic partnerships with likeminded forces in the region and committed governments around the world. Unfortunately, U.S. policy has since operated in the opposite direction. Instead of designating the ideology of the Jihadists, Washington abruptly withdrew from the war if ideas and asserted that the root cause of this particular terror movement is not embedded in an ideology, but in socioeconomic disparities. Over the years, such assertions were proven wrong, but U.S. policy continued to pull away from the ideological battlefield. In addition, the current administration decided to partner with what it described as "moderate Islamists," such as the Muslim Brotherhood, to stem the tide of what it coined as "violent extremists." But the so-called Arab Spring's upheaval—particularly in Egypt, Tunisia and Libya—has revealed a reality in conflict with the administration's assumptions. The silent majority of Arab societies and Iran opposes the Islamists as an alternative to both dictators and Jihadists. Regular people in these countries, who rarely express themselves and had it not been for the social media revolution may still have no voice, wish to move forward in their daily lives, catch up with the modernizing world, and are looking forward to obtaining a brighter future than the dark ages promised by both Jihadists and Islamists.

Last March, in 2014, I published my latest book *The Lost Spring: US Policy in the Middle East and Catastrophes to Avoid* in which I urged the U.S. administration to change course in its counterterrorism and Middle East policies in order to avoid forthcoming catastrophes, particularly in Iraq, where I urged a containment of Iran's influence before the Jihadists could seize the Sunni resistance, and in Syria, where I urged identifying an alternative opposition before a wider Jihadist takeover of the anti-regime zones; in Libya, I recommended an early backing of anti-Jihadist forces led by General Khalifa Haftar; in Egypt, I suggested rebuilding bridges with the country nascent civil society forces which unleashed the 33 million people demonstration of 2013; and last but not least, I suggested a preemptive policy in Yemen to contain the pro-Iranian militias in the north while striking at al Qaeda in the south. Regrettably, these policies never emerged and the Middle East exploded in June of 2014, producing the most dangerous terror creature to date, the Islamic State, and as a result of the latter's rise, Iran has been emboldened to stretch its influence across the region. Following are the four findings I wish to present in this testimony.

First: The Jihadi ideology of the Islamic State: Its roots and evolution

Is the ideology displayed and referred to by the Islamic State (IS) when it wages its blitzkriegs, commits its murders, and practices ethnic cleansing and sexual slavery a new ideology? In view of its own statements and references and in view of narratives previously expressed by al Qaeda, Boku Haram, Shabab, and Salafi Jihadi combat groups, the bulk of IS ideology, which portrays itself as Takfiri Salafi Jihadi, is the same ideology as that of its predecessors. The theological and historical references are identical to the modern era Jihadi groups' thinking, which finds its roots in Salafi paradigms produced earlier by thinkers from the Muslim Brotherhood movement, particularly Sayid Qutb and before him Hassan Banna, and from Wahabi narratives such as the writings of Sheikh al Albani and Ibn Uthaimin. This entire chain of radical ideological thinking derives itself from the Salafism pioneered by 18th century ideologues such as Mohammad Abdul Wahab or even medieval commentators like Ibn Taymiya. Immediately preceding ISIS's violent discourse, al Qaeda's own narrative, exemplified with texts such as the one posted online a decade ago by Abu Masaab al Suri and the manifesto published by Abu Bakr Naji —*The Management of Savagery*—or the more coherent publication *Inspire Magazine*, influenced by cleric al Awlaki in Yemen, all of this abundant Jihadi literature, seems to be more of a constant repetition of well-known Jihadi doctrines and the ideological uttering of a common core agenda. The question is what has really changed with ISIS? Was it the substance or the form?

In fact, the difference is neither the texts nor the style, but rather the geopolitical reality the Islamic State militia has been able to create on the ground. The overarching call for a new Caliphate has been uttered by ideologues in the 1920s, immediately after the fall of the Ottoman Caliphate. The Jihadi struggle during the Cold War was legitimized by the likes of Abdallah Azzam, and anti-apostate movements were active in the 1980s in Egypt with the Gamaa Islamiya. In the 1990s, ISIS-like savagery and extreme statements were witnessed in Algeria at the hands of the GIA and the GSPC. The naming of Jews and Christians as infidels and crusaders was an integral part of Osama bin Laden's two declarations of war in 1996 and 1998, and before him, the anti-American ranting of Sheikh Abdurrahman, known as "the blind Sheikh," led to the first New York bombing of 1993. From 9/11 on, calls to murder infidels, bleed economies, and establish Islamist emirates and eventually a Caliphate have been increasing, culminating in ISIS's self-declaration as the ultimate Jihadi project on the planet as of June-August 2014. In a historic sense, ISIS is not a new Jihadist movement, but the ultimate organization produced by the global Jihadist movement.

There are two mutations that distinguish the ideological product of ISIS from its predecessors. First is the fact that this terror group has achieved on the ground what has before been simply the the goals and dreams of past Jihadi groups. Its flags are flying over large cities in the Levant; its forces have withstood the power of multiple armies and of the greatest powers, at least so far; and its reach has gone farther than any previous group into many other countries. Second, and most importantly, because of the evolution of online capacities and technology, it can globally share more of its activities and thus recruit more elements. This also impresses our public even more because individuals around the world can see the atrocities, in graphic detail, as never before. Jihadists have perpetrated massacres, slaughters, ethnic cleansings and enslavement for years, particularly in south Sudan, Darfur, Nigeria and Afghanistan, to name a few, but Americans and the West did not have the access needed to personally witness these atrocities before the advent of social media, including YouTube, Facebook and others. What has really changed? We can witness the results of this ideology in detail.

Second: The geopolitical reality of an unchecked ISIS: Going global

If ISIS is not defeated strategically, both on the ground and ideologically, it will expand to much larger dimensions despite any setbacks and losses. The group had initially morphed from a hard core chapter of al Qaeda in Iraq, migrated to Syria to recruit from another al Qaeda linked group, al Ansar, and then conducted a massive blitzkrieg in Iraq last June to secure a vast adjacent territory stretching from Mosul in Iraq to Reqqa in Syria. The Islamic State forces are acquiring and losing territory in both countries but are maintaining a generally central zone across the space between Iraq and Syria. If that core area is not entirely liberated by the international coalition and transformed into a free zone for its inhabitants, ISIS will consolidate in the Levant, expand regionally and go global.

While the organization may lose some territory, as was the case in Tikrit, it is eying a multitude of other villages, towns and regions in three countries. In Iraq, ISIS is still pushing to capture Sunni districts or recapture liberated areas if the population does not feel safe with the new military occupiers. In Syria, ISIS has its designs on Sunni territories in the north, center and south, even if it would have to grab them from Jihadi competitors such as al Nusra. But the Islamic State is also determined to seize Kurdish and Christian areas in northeastern Syria and reach the Turkish borders in the north. Beyond Syria, ISIS has its designs on Tripoli in northern Lebanon and on other Sunni enclaves in the country. Once the Levantine possessions of ISIS are consolidated, efforts would head toward other emirates under construction as in Sinai, eastern Libya, several spots in the Sahel, and northern Nigeria. Somalia and Yemen, though their current Jihadi groups are allied to al Qaeda, may also start switching to ISIS. Last but not least, the open spaces of Afghanistan and Pakistan, as well as central Asia, will witness a growing ISIS presence. In my view, the adhesion to this organization is not and will not be due to the attractiveness of its current leadership, but to the power of application its ideology has accumulated by simply winning the battle.

Another, just as perturbing, consequence of an ISIS survival and growth in the region would be the magnet effect it is and would be having on Western-based Jihadists, should they be lone wolves or groups of terrorists, whether aspirant or already engaged. There is nothing like success and the sight of an "operational Caliphate" that draws the formal adherence of individuals in the West who have already been indoctrinated. If no efforts are produced to stem the expansion of the ideology in the free world and ISIS continues to send its powerful messages from the ground, a rise in recruits should be expected to reach to unparalleled levels. The travel of apprentice Jihadists to the "lands of the Caliphate" will not be the most dangerous phenomenon, rather the multiplication of Jihadists within the West would become the strategic menace, as was demonstrated in the United States, Canada, Australia, the United Kingdom, and particularly in France—with the Charlie Hebdo bloodshed.

Third: The geopolitical problems in fighting ISIS: Iran and the U.S.

If failing to stop ISIS becomes the launch pad for a much greater and aggressive threat, what are the impeding problems facing the international coalition as it is fighting the Jihadi power? We can identify two major obstructions to a strategic reversal of ISIS's expansion. One is the absence of a counter ideological strategy. By refusing to identify the Jihadi ideology, we cannot develop any significant war of ideas that can dismantle and defeat the machine producing waves of militants. The current "counter extremism" efforts by the U.S. administration are barely a nuisance to ISIS as attested to by many experts and by most Arab governments in the region. If Washington refuses to acknowledge the mere existence of a comprehensive Jihadi ideology, it deprives itself of any strategy to stop the recruitment of the enemy. For by retreating from the ideological battlefield, the U.S. is disorienting its own defense and national security capabilities as well as those of potential allies. When we don't state the doctrinal and geopolitical goals of the enemy, it becomes impossible to mobilize against the latter, neither within the region's societies nor within the homelands in the West. The antidote necessary to win the war of ideas is currently unavailable until this policy changes its course.

The second challenge the coalition has in the fight against ISIS, stems from wrong partnerships, particularly with other Islamist movements and with the Islamic Republic of Iran. For when we partner with other Islamist groups to fight ISIS, we cannot control the ideological message of these groups. By backing them, we are indirectly providing ammunition to ISIS, which has demonstrated it can recruit from the ranks of its competitors, such as al Nusra and the Muslim Brotherhood.

More dangerous is to openly partner with Iranian backed governments and militias, as is the case in Iraq. Any advance by pro-Iranian forces into ISIS territory will further radicalize the Sunnis and fuel the next uprising against the Iraqi government, let alone the risks of ethnic cleansing and suppression conducted by Shia radicals against Sunni populations. Note that what opened the path for an ISIS success in Iraq were the suppressive policies of the Maliki regime and its Iranian allies. Repeating another Iranian-backed thrust into Sunni areas in Iraq, or anywhere else under the aegis of combating ISIS, will backfire and prepare the ground for a neo-ISIS movement, one that is even more brutal that the current manifestation. Thus we recommend reshaping the struggle against the Jihadi network away from partnerships with Sunni Islamists and Shia radicals backed by Iran.

Fourth Part: Alternative strategies for the U.S. and the coalition

Based on the previous sections of this testimony, I hereby offer the following suggestions for alternative U.S. and international strategies regarding the campaign against ISIS.

1. A new war of ideas directed at Jihadism

The United States Congress can and should restructure the war with ISIS by reorganizing U.S. resources in the war of ideas. The goals of such an effort include officially identifying the ideology animating ISIS and its Jihadi allies around the world:
  (a) enabling the American public and, with the assistance of other legislatures worldwide, the wider Western public, to be aware of such ideology;
  (b) sending a message to the communities where ISIS is currently active and those where it is planning on penetrating, particularly in the Arab and Muslim world, that the U.S. and the international community have been able to isolate this ideology from civil societies' natural drive towards freedom and moderation; and
  (c) creating an international intellectual consensus against Jihadism.

In order to wage such a campaign, we strongly recommend that Congress organizes a bipartisan entity with the sole mission to build on the 9/11 Commission's recommendations and add new, more strategic and more specific material and guidelines based on the past decade of ideological evolution and from fresh input from around the world.

For this endeavor we urge Congress to hold a series of hearings on Jihadism, both the ideology and its strategies, and invite a wide array of national and international experts, but also public figures, from many countries targeted by ISIS and its Jihadi allies. For this purpose it would be important, particularly in order to dismiss the false charges of political Islamophobia, to invite the highest authority of Sunni Islam, Grand Imam of al Azhar Sheikh Ahmad al Tayyeb, to address Congress, along with a number of Muslim clerics who have publically testified against the very indoctrination machine producing the terrorists. Let Congress uncover the truth of this machine in front of the eyes of the U.S. public and international community. Moreover, we suggest Congress invite leaders from the Middle East who have been and are ideologically confronting ISIS forces, such as President Sisi of Egypt, President Sebti of Tunisia, King Abdallah of Jordan, Iraqi Kurdistan President Barazani, General Haftar of Libya, members of legislatures in the region as well as experts on Jihadism from Russia, India, China, NATO, and the African Union, in addition to members of democracy NGOs and democracy opposition movements in Iran, Syria, Lebanon, and other countries.

If Congress designates the Jihadi ideology as the chief responsible factor behind ISIS and other Jihadi terror groups, it could trigger the formation of the largest international consensus on the ideological threat and thus help this and the next U.S. administration concentrate its efforts in the right direction.

2. A new strategic coalition against ISIS

Based on the above suggestion, Congress should develop guidelines for the administration regarding a new strategic coalition against ISIS with the purpose of countering the ideology, seizing territory from ISIS, while denying the takeover of these territories by other Islamist militants or by the Iranian regime. The new strategy of the United States must insure the inclusion of several partners, each at their levels by:

(a) Consolidating a US/Western alliance with the emerging Arab Military Force and extending support to the latter's campaign in Yemen while extending a similar support to that regional force should it move to Libya, Syria and Iraq to contain and reverse the control of ISIS.
(b) Developing a new doctrine on liberating territories from ISIS by insuring that Sunni zones in Iraq and Syria be liberated by an Arab Sunni moderate force and minorities areas in both countries are put under international protection.
(c) Announcing a new vision for a post ISIS era in the Levant and around the world in order to renew the U.S. promise from WWI and WWII that no communities should again fall under sectarian, regional or ideological oppression.

Conclusion

The battle against ISIS is not simply a confrontation against that organization per se and a return to the status quo ante, but the battle must include an American, Western, and international effort to free the populations now occupied and threatened by Jihadist domination and enabling these populations and countries to remain free and to develop their own national destiny, away from all radical ambitions.

Mr. POE. Thank you, Dr. Phares. I let you go a little longer. I need time for the members to ask questions as well to both of the witnesses. But I thank you for your testimony—Ms. Rajavi, your testimony as well.

I will recognize myself for questions. How is ISIS philosophy different from Sunnis', say, in Saudi Arabia or Shi'ites' in Iran? First you, Dr. Phares, briefly.

Mr. PHARES. Well, a first difference between all Sunni Salafis on one hand and then the Shi'ite jihadists, those that Madam Rajavi has mentioned, meaning the Iranian regime and the path they are on, they both want the establishment of an international universal Islamic empire with different names.

While the Salafis in general choose the caliphate, the Khomeinis use the imamate for historical reasons that we don't probably have the time to go over.

But between ISIS and between the Saudis, the Saudis accept they are Salafi in their essence but do accept the international system. They have Ambassadors.

They accept the United Nations, they accept a minimum of consensus while ISIS doesn't accept borders, doesn't accept the existence of the international system and their acts are a result of that.

Mr. POE. Ms. Rajavi, same question. How does ISIS philosophy differ from the Sunnis in Saudi Arabia or Shi'ites in Iran?

[The following testimony was delivered through an interpreter.]

Ms. RAJAVI. So far as the formation of ISIS is concerned, it was also the mullahs' regime which helped the creation of ISIS. The crimes committed by the Iranian regime and Assad and the killing of the Sunnis in Iraq helped the emergence of ISIS.

Therefore, gaining state power, and it was the Iranian regime when there was a state in Iran, created the terrorism as a major threat for security.

But from a philosophical respect, the most fundamental element in all fundamentalist groups, whether Sunni or Shi'a, they are common on the following.

They want to force their religion or school of thought, establish a religious dictatorship whether under the name of caliphate or the absolute rule of the clergy; they do not believe in any borders and going after expansion and capturing other territories and also believe that those who do not accept the Sharia law must be eliminated.

And I want to stress that there is an antithesis to this philosophy and that is a tolerant and democratic interpretation of Islam. There is a conflict between ISIS and the mullahs in Iran but that is an internal power struggle.

But despite any differences, the continuation of other fundamentalist groups very much hinges on the Iranian regime being in power, remaining in power. Terrorism and fundamentalism under the name of Islam came to the world scene by the mullahs' regime in Iran and when this regime is overthrown that will be limited or destroyed.

And it is interesting that after the emergence of ISIS the people of Iran called the Iran regime, the godfather of ISIS. Regarding Saudi Arabia, I want to add that ISIS, contrary to Saudi Arabia, they do not believe in borders. Therefore, the question is not being Sunni or Salafi or whatever.

The problem is those characteristics which I just identified and that is where you will see that despite all the differences ISIS is very close to the fundamentalist ruling in Iran. Thank you.

Mr. POE. Ms. Rajavi, may I ask you a question that you made a comment about? How do you see the mullahs in Iran having facilitated and helped the ISIS movement?

How has ISIS been able to expand its influence, its philosophy because of the mullahs in Iran? Make that clear, if you would, on how there is that connection.

Ms. RAJAVI. As I said, there is a power struggle between ISIS and the regime. But at the same time, on occasions they have cooperated.

For example, Zarqawi, the original founder and leader of ISIS, received enormous logistic support from the Iranian regime and had his bases even in Iran. And I think it was in 2005 that intelligence security services in Germany exposed this connection between Zarqawi and the Iranian regime.

And also there has been many reports even in the media that Bashar al-Assad released many of the ISIS members from prison in order to join ISIS. While in their air attacks they have never attacked ISIS but the focus is on the moderate opposition in Syria.

So I want to conclude that so far as the mullah's regime in Iran is concerned, they are 100 percent supporting Bashar al-Assad in Syria and therefore all the crimes that are committed by the help and support of the mullah's regime has created a fertile ground for ISIS to emerge.

And on the other hand, crimes committed by Maliki at the behest of the Iranian regime in Iraq and in particular the absolute suppression of the Sunnis has led to empowering ISIS to expand itself both in Iraq and Syria.

Mr. POE. I will yield 5 minutes to the ranking member from Massachusetts, Mr. Keating.

Mr. KEATING. Thank you, Mr. Chairman.

I want to follow up on Ambassador Ford's testimony in terms of Dr. Phares. I really want to see if we can get to the root of some things, as short as this time is.

Your main thought was that the ideology is the controlling factor—absolute controlling factor that happens. Is that correct? I think I got that.

Mr. PHARES. The ideology is what produces them but it is not the only element that controls their action. But without the ideology they cannot be produced. So the movement can use this pool only if it exists.

Mr. KEATING. So the leaders would be pure to that ideology?

Mr. PHARES. Yes. The leaders who are produced by this movement, if they are eliminated, that would slow down the activity of the movement.

Mr. KEATING. Then here is where I have the problem trying to put everything—it is nice to put everything in one box. I wish we could in this instance.

But if it was absolutely controlling, how do you explain then that ISIL will then take cultural artifacts and it will destroy them because they are uncompromising, as Ambassador Ford said?

And they are ideologically centered, so they are destroying those cultural artifacts that aren't inconsistent with their ideological beliefs. But if they are so pure why are they taking these things then and selling them, preserving them to get money?

Isn't that more the actions of a criminal enterprise too? I mean, it is not as simple. It is complex and I think that is part of it.

If we focus on one narrow box we are going to miss the whole picture. But there is an element of that, isn't there, with ISIL?

Mr. PHARES. Mr. Congressman, I think it is the other way around. If I may not disagree but readjust the argument. In past similar situations with totalitarian armies that were supposed to go only by ideology, and I am talking about World War II, should it be the Nazi armies or the Soviet armies, you can't get more totalitarian and disciplined, they have done the same.

Rank and file could go against the ideology and the instructions that are——

Mr. KEATING. These are the leaders that are making these decisions.

Mr. PHARES. The leaders of the ISIS movement can also be corrupt. There is no doubt about it, and there were leaders in the Communist movement in the past during the Cold War and guerilla forces that were corrupt.

My point is, we have to give what to Caesar is to Caesar and, of course, what the corrupt are doing is their natural behavior. I am not claiming that the ideology will only produce a perfect behavior.

But what I am claiming is that without the ideology you cannot have jihadists. Then another argument would win.

Mr. KEATING. But there is——they are related and they can't, I don't think, be ignored. Ambassador Ford——I am sorry you weren't here and thank you for coming and making the trouble with plane flights and all——but Ambassador Ford, upon being pressed in questioning, became clear there are other social factors that are a part of this and to me, the chairman's experience in law enforcement as a judge, mine as a prosecutor, there are social issues that breed criminal activity.

It is not——there are people in the same social settings with the same challenges. They don't become criminals. But there are some that are.

Mr. PHARES. That is true.

Mr. KEATING. And more so than not and you can't say that that is not a factor even. So I think the social conditions——and I am sorry you weren't here to see——hear Ambassador Ford's testimony—— but they are a factor as well. It is not pure ideology.

And I don't deny there is ideology. That is a given.

Mr. PHARES. I hear you, Congressman. There is a point, of course, in socioeconomics for everything else, not just for the jihadists but for every ultra nationalist movement.

Let me draw your attention to the fact that Egypt in 2013, while the argument was that people were adhering to the Muslim Brotherhood because they were not finding jobs or because of the social conditions, when on June 30th, 2013, 33 million Egyptians, 80 percent of whom are under the level of poverty, marched against the Muslim Brotherhood, that defeats the logic that it is only socioeconomic. But I do agree with you that socioeconomics are part of it.

Mr. KEATING. That is important because I think if we are going to fight them we have to fight them in so many different levels.

And one of the things you brought up that I thought was very important was our messaging and how we can do a better job messaging, and I think we have to incorporate the Muslim community back home and have their voices be trusted voices in opposition.

But if you could comment just briefly on what we could do not only in the U.S. but in Europe and Turkey, you know, in approaching this problem. I gave you a lot in a short time so I am sorry.

Mr. PHARES. Absolutely. Thank you again.

I did 5 years of research on our messaging, both administrations, the bureaucracy in general. The problem is, first of all, we have to vet who we are working with in terms of message, meaning we need to work with NGOs who have had an experience on the ground in the region and have an experience here and can be diverse as much as possible.

Even within our own communities when we are dealing with organizations, we cannot say this one organization represents the entire community unless we have referendums in this country, which I don't think under the Constitution we do.

So I agree fully with you the next stage to push back against radicalization is from within these communities to have NGOs that are vetted and that they are willing to push back against the doctrine.

Mr. KEATING. Thank you. I am over my time but I think this is a crucial issue that we have to address. Thank you.

Mr. POE. The Chair recognizes the gentleman from New York, Mr. Zeldin.

Mr. ZELDIN. Thank you, Mr. Chairman.

Mr. Keating was just asking about the socioeconomics. My question—I just want to get to the heart, Doctor, of what is the most effective way to get inside the head of ISIS and demoralize them?

Mr. PHARES. Well, that is a different battle, Mr. Congressman, from the interception I suggested but I will answer both.

Pushing back against an individual who has already been radicalized is a much bigger mission. It would need a much larger mobilization.

It needs for ISIS elements to feel that the people are against them and that the international community in the region are against them, so in response to what the congressman has mentioned about strategic communication, we need to do a better job.

Our Arab broadcast, our Persian broadcast, that the Congress funds here, has not been doing, in my own view, enough to push back against these organizations.

But I do propose that before these individuals are radicalized, this is where we need to interfere. When kids are 10 and 12 and 13, in a short 10 years, as in Afghanistan or as in Iraq and in Syria, they are the new ISIS.

So we need to add and supply strategies that would help first women, their mothers and teachers, and the NGOs to be part of this enterprise, not just on the military level, not just on the economic level, but on the educational level.

Mr. ZELDIN. What is the most effective way, though, for those who are currently part of ISIS who are beheading individuals in their region—what is the best way to get into the head of ISIS and demoralize them?

Mr. PHARES. Congressman, it is only a massive military defeat of large areas controlled by ISIS.

Mr. ZELDIN. Thank you. I mean, I totally agree with you. I mean, we could spend a lot of time here, you know, talking about other elements of what we are up against and we can spend—we can have a hearing dedicated to talking about social economics.

We can all admit that maybe there is something to do with the economy. That might have something to do with it. But the best way to get into the head of a member of ISIS is to put a round in it—is with lead.

Honestly, they have to be defeated. That is what we are up against. And we can have a tremendous amount of patience waiting for someone else to fill this vacuum and step up in the region.

But listen, when you want to be the leader of the free world, you know, American exceptionalism isn't about figuring out a way to get everyone a job. You know, King Abdul of Jordan, you know, when one of their pilots is executed isn't filming a video to ISIS and the rest of the world on how we need to get them more jobs.

You know, Israeli Prime Minister Benjamin Netanyahu, when he is giving a speech about, you know, what we do with our enemies around the world it is not that we need to give them more wealth.

I mean, we have to confront this threat and, honestly, if you want to—if you want to demoralize them, if you want to defeat ISIS—it is not going to be done through social programs of giving people jobs and more wealth.

The world needs America to lead. Now, it is our responsibility here to ensure that we are never setting our services members up to defeat. I do not support occupations, enduring ground operations.

But there is a big difference when you are talking about Navy SEALS, Delta Force, Green Berets, Marines, Army Rangers who in the middle of the night under the cover of darkness they are going to show up at areas where ISIS is operating, where ISIS is sleeping, and they are going to execute well-planned missions that is going to take out high-value targets and capture actionable intelligence.

Our enemies do not respect weakness. They only respect strength, and strength cannot be shown just by finding jobs for more people who are members of ISIS. It is—it is divorced from reality to spend time here talking about social economics as if that is the root of what we are up against and that is the way to turn the tide.

You know, we are all saying it is all part of it. That might be why some people are getting involved in ISIS. It might have something to do with economics. That is not going to eliminate the threat.

Now, Madam Rajavi, listening to you speak and mentioning the Green Revolution back in 2009, and we think about the undemocratic elections that took place in Iran, at that point when the economy was doing better and oil was $100 a barrel, and millions of Iranians were rising up to take control of their country, and our President was saying that that was none of our problem.

Fast forward today when the economy is worse and oil is $50 a barrel and people like you are showing a leadership, willing to take control of your own destiny.

I honestly do not know whether or not my President is on the same exact team that I am because there are individuals like you who are willing to rise up and take control of your country's future and destiny with a vision, whether it is Iran or Syria or elsewhere, to bring stability to the Middle East.

I commend you for being here and for leading your effort. I yield back the balance of my time.

Mr. POE. The gentleman yields back.

The Chair recognizes the gentleman from California for 5 minutes.

Mr. SHERMAN. Thank you, Mr. Chairman. I agree with the last gentleman and point out that on the issue of socioeconomics not being the driving force, keep in mind 19 of the 20 hijackers on 9/11 were from a rich oil-rich country and were middle class in their background. They did not take over those planes because they couldn't support their families.

This hearing is about defining the enemy and the President is attacked by some because he doesn't have the courage to give ISIS the ideological victory that ISIS wants. ISIS wants to be called the Islamic State.

They want to be regarded as Islamic. They want to be regarded as a state. I think they are heretic terrorists, not Islamic scholar statesmen, and so I do not think the President should be criticized for not calling them Islamic when they are heretics, and not calling them a state when they are terrorists.

Also, the topic of this hearing is defining the enemy and I think the greatest enemy is the Shi'ite alliance. I have said that before in this room, the alliance of Iran, Assad, Hezbollah, now the Houthi, has killed more Muslims, killed more Americans and poses a greater threat of mass destruction than does ISIS.

I am glad to have Ms. Rajavi here. I want to thank the MEK for revealing to the world the Natanz nuclear plant. There may have been a few members of the intel committee who knew that before the MEK told us.

But speaking on behalf of roughly 400 Members of Congress, thank you for telling Congress as well.

Now, you personally promote a very tolerant moderate view of Islam. You are an advocate of the separation of religion and state, and you have been an advocate for human rights and women's rights.

Of course, your country is ruled by very rigid laws that call for stoning people and chopping off limbs. ISIS does the same thing supposedly in support of a different version of Islam—Iran being Shi'ite, ISIS being Sunni.

Why is their understanding of Islam the same, or at least similar to our eyes, and why do both the rulers of Iran and ISIS enforce their beliefs through these gruesome measures? If you could respond.

I am sorry. We are unable to hear you. I don't know if our——

Mr. POE. Technical difficulty here.

Mr. SHERMAN [continuing]. Technical people can help that.

Ms. RAJAVI. Thank you very much, Congressman Sherman. You touched upon a very important issue. You said that Islamic fundamentalism of the kind of the Shi'ite is even more dangerous than the Sunni one before anything else.

The reason is that there is a state empowered in the dimension of the mullahs' regime in a country—in a vast country with so many resources—financial resources—and it is supporting these Shi'ite fundamentalist groups financially, ideologically and logistically in every field.

Therefore, they are much more dangerous. I agree with you. Regarding your question as to why they resort to so much violence to pursue their objectives I should tell you that the reason is they can only survive through absolute terror and fear, and this has been the trend of over 30 years of ruling fundamentalists in Iran that now has expanded to Iraq, Syria, Yemen, Lebanon and other countries, and other fundamentalists take lessons from the Godfather.

Let us not forget that the mullahs in Iran are implementing more than 70 kind of different tortures—cutting off limbs or gauging eyes, executing pregnant women and all the heinous crimes that one might imagine—and now ISIS and other fundamentalists are really imitating from the mullahs in Iran.

Therefore, I reiterate once again that the ultimate solution is, one, evict, dislodge the Iranian regime from Syria and Iraq and Yemen and, even more important, regime change in Iran.

The fundamentalist regime in Iran must be changed because this regime has created a political umbrella and a source of ideology and logistical and financial support for the fundamentalists and terrorists in today's world.

If it were not due to the destructive influence of the Iranian regime, we would not face the situation today in Iraq, Yemen and Syria and they would have stability.

Let us not forget that by regime change in Iran, those militia under the command of the Quds Force, like the Hezbollah in Lebanon or Ansar Allah of the Houthis in Yemen, and other various groups in Iraq, would be eliminated without having their support and they would not have the vital environment to survive.

Mr. POE. Does the gentleman yield back his time?

Mr. SHERMAN. I would love to ask another question but I have gone over. I yield back.

Mr. POE. The Chair recognizes the gentleman from New York, Mr. Higgins.

Mr. HIGGINS. Thank you, Mr. Chairman.

Doctor, you had—we got called out for votes—but you were making three points when I came in, and number two was you made reference to ideological confrontation I presume toward the goal to delegitimize ISIS. Could you elaborate further?

Mr. PHARES. Thank you, Mr. Congressman.

The first goal is to delegitimize them but there is a more important goal. It is to encourage and mobilize civil societies where ISIS controls so eventually, when ISIS control is eliminated by military means, there will be no new ISIS.

My whole point to the panel is that ISIS is a new al-Qaeda, al-Qaeda a new Ansar al-Sharia. These are organizations. Every time there is a problem and a suppression, they come back.

So the ideological battle is not just to deter them. It is to create a resistance inside these societies to make it impossible for a new ISIS to emerge.

Mr. HIGGINS. So you have to confront the ideology in order to stop the evolution of these groups from proliferating. So how is that done?

Mr. PHARES. It is done in the field where it has been fought. The message that ISIS and the jihadists are producing and, of course, sending through Internet and—the problem is not Internet and Facebook—the problem is who is responding to them. We need to partner with and work with leaders and ideologues such as the spiritual leader of Sunni Islam. I just came back from Egypt a few weeks ago.

I met with Sheikh Azhar, the equivalent of the Sunni Pope. We had a long conversation. He is ready to mobilize against this way of thinking.

There are many clerics around the Muslim world. They are ready to move. Their problem—there is no coordination among themselves and us.

Mr. HIGGINS. With all due respect, we hear this all the time but it never happens. You know, the United States, whether you agreed with our involvement in Iraq, you know, the best that we could hope for was taking out a bad guy and creating a breathing space within which Shi'a, Sunni and Kurds could develop some kind of social contract and live peacefully amongst one another.

Obviously, that didn't happen. You know, some would say that ISIS is just trying to get their country back in Iraq because the origins of ISIS, clearly, are de-Baathification and the dissolution of the Iraq army under Saddam Hussein, who were Sunnis.

And maybe it is second generation, but as you talk about the continuum of this kind of extremist activity, their roots are somewhere. I suppose the question is, you know, where is the end and how do you achieve that?

You also said that jihadis become jihadis by indoctrination and I know there was some discussion here about whether or not socio-economic factors contribute to that.

I suppose they do to a degree. That is certainly not the only vulnerability to radicalization. But I would suggest—I would argue that some of it is.

You know, I think the American people become very frustrated because we, as the indispensable nation, are called upon to try to intervene to resolve these problems. But yet at its core, these problems have to be resolved internally, and the Middle East is a very pluralistic society.

There is a very pluralistic society. But there is a zero sum game mentality and in order for somebody to win somebody has to lose.

And that is why Bashar al-Assad in Syria enjoys partnerships with people he has no interest in.

Just because they are minorities, the Sunnis take over, they feel as though they will get slaughtered and therefore they align themselves with Bashar al-Assad so that they don't get slaughtered.

There is no recognition of minority rights. You know, in game theory there is also what is referred to as a variable sum game and that means that there can be multiple winners. But in order to promote a peaceful path toward an existence of peaceful coexistence there has to be pretty profound compromises.

You know, I referenced before in Northern Ireland they had a history—a horrible history of Protestants and Catholics killing each other. No troops were deployed by the United States in Northern Ireland.

But both sides, in order to participate in the Good Friday Agreement of 1998, had to denounce violence publicly—paramilitaries on both sides—the Irish Republican Army and the Protestant paramilitaries—and they actually had to participate in the destruction of their arms with an international tribunal.

And, you know, my point is you are either going to get democracy through peaceful means or, in the absence of that, civil war. And the United States fought a civil war where 650,000 to 700,000 people were killed at a time where our country's population was about 30 million people.

I mean, that is very, very significant. But that is the consequence of not being able to resolve your problems peacefully. So as we, you know, look for solutions with these very clear maps of delineation as to who is responsible, but this is—you know, this is probably pretty accurate. There is a lot of duplicity going on there.

You know, Tom Friedman, the author and New York Times columnist, once said, "Is Iraq the way it is because Saddam is the way he is, or is Saddam the way he is because Iraq is the way it is?"

And I think unless and until these Middle Eastern countries recognize, you know, that there is something beyond the horizon than hating one another and killing each other in the name of God then we are just going to be at this table and these panels for years and years to come.

There has got to be some enlightenment and that is going to require leadership, and it is going to require leadership in the Arab Muslim world.

Mr. POE. And you yield back your time. And without objection, this chart that was hastily made by the Chair, will be made part of the record and with—I ask unanimous consent that Mr. Davis, who is not a member of this committee, be allowed to ask questions and if there is no objection then the Chair recognizes Mr. Davis from Illinois.

Mr. DAVIS. Thank you very much, Mr. Chairman, and I want to thank you for your indulgence. Indeed, I am not a member of this subcommittee but I do have interest in the subject matter, and I want to thank you and I thank both of our witnesses for being here.

Ms. Rajavi, over the past 30 years the United States has been drawn into some serious diplomatic and military dead ends in the Mideast by mistakenly backing individuals and organizations claiming popular support which turned out to be largely exaggerated and somewhat manufactured.

Would you please tell us about the role of the National Council of Resistance in Iranian civil life and its place in current Iranian political life, and how do you measure your popular support in Iran?

Ms. RAJAVI. With absolute repression it is not possible to go to the vote of people and see what the people really think, and the mullahs will never accept a free election.

Therefore, the yardstick or the gage for the popularity of this movement, one, is its persistent continuation of its principles despite the absolute repression and having lost 120,000 of its members and sympathizers who were executed by the regime.

I show you now this book, which includes the names of some 20,000 members of the resistance movement from different strata of the Iranian society. So you can imagine that collecting such information during repression is very difficult.

But another indication is the fear of the regime and its engagement in demonizing the Iranian resistance as another indication of the strength of the resistance and its popularity.

As you may know, in all the diplomatic correspondence that they have their main demands from their interlocutors is to restrict the activities of our movement and any affiliation with our movement in Iran is equal to execution.

In the 2009 uprising, the regime's officials acknowledged publicly that those demonstrations were organized by a Mujahideen network, the MEK network in Iran, and this popular support has enabled this movement also to have access to most secret information of the Iranian regime—on nuclear, on missile and what the Quds Force is doing in the region as well as the human rights violations in Iran.

We have always said to the mullahs' regime that if you really claim that our movement has no popular support, let us have a free election under the auspices of the international community and let us see who has the popular support of the Iranian people. But let us not forget that a free election for the mullahs is a red line.

Mr. DAVIS. Thank you very much.

Dr. Phares, do you believe that the United States should be cooperating militarily with Iran in combating ISIS in Iraq and Syria, and if yes, how and to what extent? Is it direct cooperation or indirect cooperation through the Iraqi Government and if no, why not?

Mr. PHARES. Well, I will begin by the answer no, and certainly no, Mr. Congressman. I will give the argument that unless there is a change in the government and in the direction, at least, of Iranian policy in the region, cooperating with the regime that is waging a campaign in Iraq, in Syria, in Lebanon and now in Yemen against five or seven of our own allies and probably soon to be trying to destabilize Bahrain, it would be a strategic mistake.

So I am not against the principle that the United States would cooperate with anybody to defeat the terrorists. But if we cooperate with the Iranians as they are engaged militarily against our own allies, and there is something even more important—every inch of land taken away from ISIS, which is the good thing, all depends on who is taking away that inch from the organization.

If the Iranian-controlled militias or Iranians with different aspects in Iraq are taking over, we would be replacing one problem with another problem.

So my answer is, clearly, no to that cooperation unless we see a change or a reform and, clearly, we have not seen yet a Gorbachev-like perestroika or glasnost inside Iran for the time being.

Mr. DAVIS. Thank you very much and, Mr. Chairman, again, I thank you for your indulgence and I yield back.

Mr. POE. I thank the gentleman. Without objection, unanimous consent the Chair will allow another individual who is not a member of this committee to ask questions. Ms. Chu from California is recognized.

Ms. CHU. Thank you, Mr. Chair.

I would like to address these questions to Ms. Rajavi. I would like to ask about Camp Liberty. Camp Liberty is a military base that has become a permanent home for over 3,000 Iranian refugees.

But the conditions there are poor and freedom is very severely restricted. Worse, there are reports that the Iraqi Government is blockading the base, preventing food, water and medicine from arriving.

Combined with the restriction on travel, this blockade has led to at least 25 deaths, the most recent being Mr. Jalal Abedini on April 17th.

Can you give us a sense of living conditions in Camp Liberty in regard to food, medicine and decent housing?

Ms. RAJAVI. Our prime concern about the residents in Camp Liberty is their safety and security. That is the main problem that they are facing in Camp Liberty now to the extent that since the protection of the residents was transferred from the United States to Iraq 116 have been killed, seven have been taken hostage and the residents are denied timely access to medical care.

And for this reason, as you have just mentioned, 25 people have lost their lives while there was the possibility to save their life.

I think it was 116 who have been killed during these attacks by Iraqi forces; they have no freedom of movement and enormous restrictions have been imposed on them.

Just to give you one example, Camp Liberty's electricity is not connected to the city grid and since the Abadi government took office there has been no changes in the condition and there is still a prison-like situation for the residents.

And I think the new government must recognize Camp Liberty as a refugee camp and remove all the inhumane restrictions which have been imposed on the camp and put an end to the daily harassment of the residents.

In particular, it is very important that the camp management be changed because they are the same people—the people who are the camp management are the same people who were engaged in the massacre and the killing of the residents in the past attacks.

And as you know, the United States Government had made a written commitment to provide safety and security for these people but that obligation has been violated and I think Camp Liberty should be really put under the protection of the United States or at least their personal weapons to be given so that if they are attacked by the militias or paramilitary groups that they could defend themselves.

And I expect that the United States upholds its commitment to regular monitoring of Camp Liberty.

Ms. CHU. Let me ask now about—do you have any confidence in the current government to improve conditions and what is the future for the people at Camp Liberty? Is there a U.S. role?

Ms. RAJAVI. I think the U.S. Government can really demand and urge the Iraqi Government to uphold its obligations.

So far, the government has not done anything that we could really trust that they will do the right thing, and as I said that the people are still living in a prison-like situation in Camp Liberty as prisoners.

That is why I said that the new government should recognize Liberty as a refugee camp and remove all the restriction imposed on the camp and end the harassment of the residents.

And I want to reiterate that it is very vital to change the camp management and do not allow the mullahs' regime to send its agents for psychological torture of the residents and laying the ground for another massacre in Camp Liberty. These are actions that they can take and I believe that the United States Government is in a position to really call on and demand from the Iraqi Government to uphold this obligation.

Ms. CHU. Thank you. I yield back.

Mr. POE. I thank the gentlelady.

We have also been joined on the dais by the gentlelady from Texas, Ms. Jackson Lee, and without objection and unanimous consent that she will be allowed to question the witnesses. You have 5 minutes.

Ms. JACKSON LEE. Mr. Chairman, thank you very much for your kindness and let me add my appreciation to both you and Ranking Member Sherman and all the members on this panel for their courtesies extended and to indicate that this is a very historic hearing because as far as my memory can recollect, Mr. Chairman, this is one of the few times that the voice of the opposition of the Government of Iran has been part of an official discussion.

And that is very important for the American people and for us to formulate the right kinds of policies. Many of us worked for long years to ensure that this great leader, who happens to be a woman, would be able to speak and would be able to lead the MEK and be removed from the terrorist list.

There were many machinations and court decisions and we have moved to a decision which I think reflects the fairness of this nation. Might I also say that the importance of hearing both views in this backdrop of ISIS and the backdrop of the merging of the caliphate—it is from Syria to Iraq to Iran is very important.

As we watch Yemen, and we watch Libya, we know that we have to come together around a full understanding of the influence and impact of ISIS.

So let me say to Ms. Rajavi, who has been a continuing leader and someone who has opened her information cycle, if I will, to ensure that information be given. She doesn't hide information. She has been open and forthright.

So I would like to pose these questions. We are trying to discern ISIS the enemy and I would just make the comment that any organization that beheads and uses the kind of horrific video to intimidate certainly is a defined enemy, from my perspective, and all those who contribute to the growth and continuation of ISIS, using them as a front for the dastardly deeds they want to do, we have to review.

We have to look at Syria. We have to look at what is happening in Iraq and we certainly must look at what is happening in Iran.

But I do want to say as well in the nuclear nonproliferation agreement framework, which we don't have, I still believe that we should look at that in a way that we look and analyze first before we condemn and we take the input that Members of Congress will hopefully be able to give and we look forthright to ensure that Iraq knows—that Iraq knows we mean business but, more importantly, this agreement that may come about with Iran is to enhance the security of the United States of America.

To Ms. Rajavi, I would like to ask the question that you promote a very tolerant and moderate view of Islam. You are an advocate of separation of religion and state and you also favor women's rights and human rights.

Is it true that Iran is upholding laws that call for the stoning to death of people and the chopping off of limbs?

Can she hear that I was directing that question?

Mr. POE. There is a satellite involved in this communication and it takes a while, plus the translation.

Ms. JACKSON LEE. Thank you.

Ms. RAJAVI. Yes, precisely. I should say that what the mullahs really want under the pretext of Islam are doing—they are doing it under the pretext of Islam, but it has nothing to do with Islam.

They stone people, amputate limbs and they rape people and so far, as I said, 120,000 of the best children of the Iranian people have been executed under the name of religion and Islam.

But I should make it clear that Islam is a religion of compassion and freedom and rejects fanaticism, dogmatism and dictatorship. Congresswoman Jackson Lee as you mentioned, we believe in separation of religion and state. We advocate a tolerant and democratic interpretation of Islam, which is the genuine Islam, and we believe that it is the vote of the people that will count.

In our view, there is gender equality between men and women. While, you know that fundamentalists are misogynists and whatever is based on compulsion is contrary to Islamic teaching.

There is no compulsion in religion, in what you wear and how you think, and as the Koran said, there is no compulsion in religion. Sovereignty and the vote of people is the treatment—please, go ahead.

Ms. JACKSON LEE. Thank you. I am going to make these very brief because I know our time has ended. I just simply know that in the 1979 revolution the Iranian intellectuals called for democracy and human rights.

You just mentioned Islamic fundamentalism, which Iran seems to be the epicenter of and therefore promoting terrorism. You might want to comment how you think this happened to Iran and then maybe the top challenges that we must face.

If we identify ISIL as an enemy, what are the challenges that relate to freedom, democracy, peace and security that we all want to see? Let me finish by saying that if you have any comments about Camp Liberty and those continued attacks if you want to include that as to how we can work to better stop that, and I would appreciate the chairman's indulgence and I thank you very much for your answers to these questions.

Ms. RAJAVI. You are absolutely right. The people of Iran wanted freedom and democracy from the revolution and they continue to yearn for freedom and democracy. But, unfortunately, Khomeini stole the leadership of the revolution which was for freedom and democracy and imposed a fundamentalist regime which by eliminating all freedom and eliminating all political forces from the Iranian society, particularly women and the youth, and established its rule.

And for the past 37 years a fundamentalist government has been in power in Tehran. This regime is based on two pillars—export of terrorism and fundamentalism outside and domestic repression, and at the same time trying to acquire nuclear weapons in order to take hostage the international community for doing nothing against these atrocities.

These are the basis or the pillars of this regime. In the month of April, just in this month, nearly 150 executions have been announced in Iran. Only by absolute repression they are maintaining their power.

But on the other hand, there is—an organized resistance, which has been resisting this fundamentalist regime for the past 37 years and has been able to expose the fundamentalism and terrorism of this regime and to show the world who is the epicenter of fundamentalism in Iraq, Syria, Lebanon and Yemen and other parts of the world and to show that where are the secret sites, nuclear secret sites of the mullahs are operating and they have been operating and also to inform the world about the human rights violations in Iran.

But I am absolutely confident that the people of Iran and the Iranian resistance will bring an end and overthrow this mullahs' regime and bring freedom and democracy for the people of Iran and for the people of the whole region.

And just very briefly about Liberty, as I said, we expect that the United States Government upholds its obligations which has been violated by now and the U.S. Government must really put Camp Liberty under its own protection soon and to put an end to the blockade and to demand from the Iraqi Government to lift the blockade and to recognize their rights as a protected person under the Geneva Conventions. I thank you.

Ms. JACKSON LEE. Thank you. Thank you very much, Mr. Chairman.

Mr. POE. The gentlelady yields back her time.

Ms. JACKSON LEE. The gentlelady yields back the time. Thank you.

Mr. POE. I want to thank all of the members of the committee and guests of the committee for being here today.

This has been a very insightful hearing and the witnesses have presented three different perspectives of the problem of ISIS, starting with Ambassador Ford succinctly analyzing that they are driven by doctrine and they are driven by the philosophy that compromise is a sin.

And Dr. Phares, you brought in your expertise to say and show that this isn't just a philosophy that is against Christians and Jews but it is a philosophy that also attacks Muslims to a great deal—maybe more Muslims than other groups.

And Ms. Rajavi, I want to thank you as well, bringing a perspective from an Iranian point of view that is not the official mullah point of view of the Government of Iran, having your expertise and seeing firsthand the results of oppression in Iran and the oppression of ISIS, and thank you as well, especially this late time in the evening. I guess it is about 11:30 or 11:45 wherever, somewhere in there.

But I do also want to thank all of the people in the audience that have shown a great interest in this hearing.

So this subcommittee is adjourned and there will be follow-up questions by—that can be submitted by members of the subcommittee to all of the witnesses that have testified.

Thank you.

[Whereupon, at 5:07 p.m., the committee was adjourned.]

APPENDIX

Material Submitted for the Record

SUBCOMMITTEE HEARING NOTICE
COMMITTEE ON FOREIGN AFFAIRS
U.S. HOUSE OF REPRESENTATIVES
WASHINGTON, DC 20515-6128

Subcommittee on Terrorism, Nonproliferation, and Trade
Ted Poe (R-TX), Chairman

TO: MEMBERS OF THE COMMITTEE ON FOREIGN AFFAIRS

You are respectfully requested to attend an OPEN hearing of the Committee on Foreign Affairs, to be held by the Subcommittee on Terrorism, Nonproliferation, and Trade in Room 2172 of the Rayburn House Office Building (and available live on the Committee website at http://www.ForeignAffairs.house.gov):

DATE: Wednesday, April 29, 2015

TIME: 2:00 p.m.

SUBJECT: ISIS: Defining the Enemy

WITNESSES: Panel I
                   The Honorable Robert Ford
                   Senior Fellow
                   The Middle East Institute
                   (Former U.S. Ambassador to Syria)

                   Walid Phares, Ph.D.
                   Co-Secretary General
                   Transatlantic Parliamentary Group on Counterterrorism

                   Panel II
                   Mrs. Maryam Rajavi
                   President-Elect
                   National Council of Resistance of Iran
                   (Appearing via teleconference)

By Direction of the Chairman

The Committee on Foreign Affairs seeks to make its facilities accessible to persons with disabilities. If you are in need of special accommodations, please call 202/225-5021 at least four business days in advance of the event, whenever practicable. Questions with regard to special accommodations in general (including availability of Committee materials in alternative formats and assistive listening devices) may be directed to the Committee.

COMMITTEE ON FOREIGN AFFAIRS

MINUTES OF SUBCOMMITTEE ON _____ *Terrorism Nonproliferation and Trade* _____ HEARING

Day **Wednesday** Date **April 29, 2015** Room **2172**

Starting Time **2:00 p.m.** Ending Time **5:07 p.m.**

Recesses **1** (**3:34** to **3:54**) (___to___) (___to___) (___to___) (___to___) (___to___)

Presiding Member(s)

Chairman Ted Poe

Check all of the following that apply:

Open Session ☑
Executive (closed) Session ☐
Televised ☑

Electronically Recorded (taped) ☑
Stenographic Record ☑

TITLE OF HEARING:

"ISIS: Defining the Enemy"

SUBCOMMITTEE MEMBERS PRESENT:

Reps. Poe, Issa, Perry, Zeldin, Keating, Sherman, Higgins

NON-SUBCOMMITTEE MEMBERS PRESENT: *(Mark with an * if they are not members of full committee.)*

Reps. Jackson Lee*, Chu*, D. Davis (IL)*

HEARING WITNESSES: Same as meeting notice attached? Yes ☑ No ☐
(If "no", please list below and include title, agency, department, or organization.)

STATEMENTS FOR THE RECORD: *(List any statements submitted for the record.)*

Rep. McClintock (Statement for the Record)

TIME SCHEDULED TO RECONVENE _____
or
TIME ADJOURNED **4:00 p.m.**

Subcommittee Staff Director

MATERIAL SUBMITTED FOR THE RECORD BY THE HONORABLE TED POE, A REPRESENTA-
TIVE IN CONGRESS FROM THE STATE OF TEXAS, AND CHAIRMAN, SUBCOMMITTEE ON
TERRORISM, NONPROLIFERATION, AND TRADE

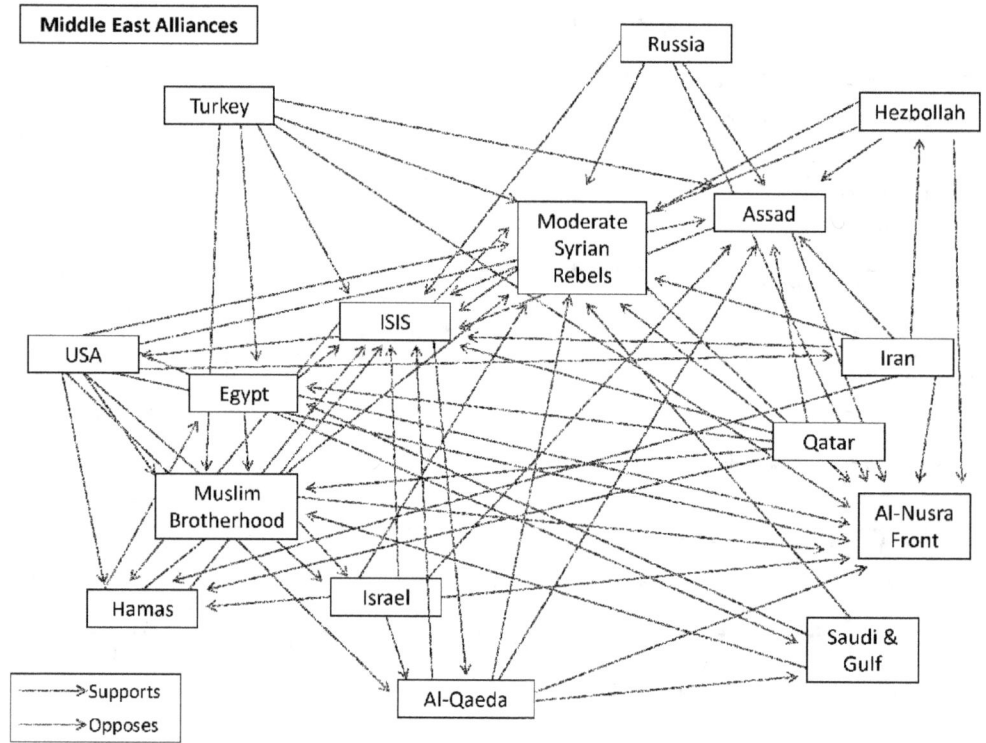

Statement for the Record from Rep. McClintock
ISIS: Defining the Enemy
Subcommittee Hearing: Subcommittee on Terrorism, Nonproliferation and Trade
2:00 PM, Wednesday, April 29, 2015

I want to thank Chairman Poe and the Subcommittee on Terrorism, Nonproliferation and Trade for holding a hearing on the critical threat that the Iranian regime presents to the world.

I am especially pleased that the Subcommittee invited as a witness Ms. Maryam Rajavi, whose movement is at the forefront of opposition to Islamic fundamentalism, offering a formidable alternative of greater freedom and tolerance in Iran and throughout the Muslim world. She and her colleagues bear much credibility as voices of democracy, as evidenced by the persecution they continue to suffer at the hands of Iran's dictators.

I want to once again thank Ms. Rajavi for testifying and express my profound admiration for her leadership and courage in liberating the Iranian people from tyranny.